Born to Rise
The Unspoken Principles Behind Power,
Riches, and Lasting Wealth
Shree Shambav

Published by Shree Shambav, Tamil Nadu, India

All Rights Reserved

First Edition, 2025

Copyright © 2025, Muniswamy Rajakumar

All rights reserved. No part of this publication may be reproduced, distributed, or transmitted in any form or by any means, including photocopying, recording, or other electronic or mechanical methods, without the author's prior written permission. It is illegal to copy this book, post it to a website, or distribute it by any other means without permission.

The request for permission should be addressed to the author.

ISBN: 978-93-343-1595-0
Email:shreeshambav@gmail.com
Web:www.shambav.org

Born to Rise

The Unspoken Principles Behind Power, Riches, and Lasting Wealth

"Rise beyond riches. Master the unseen. Live wea[lthy in] soul and self."

SHREE SHAMBAV

DEDICATION

"Isavasyam idam sarvam yat kim ca jagatyam jagat, tena tyaktena bhunjitha, ma gridhah kasyasvid dhanam"

To the Almighty,

the Divine Masters,

the family who listens,

and my parents who see –

your presence shapes the pages of my life's journey.

"Isavasyam idam sarvam yat kim ca jagatyam jagat"

Meaning: "God encompasses everything you perceive, see, or touch with your sense organs."

DISCLAIMER

This book is not a prescription—it is an invitation.

Born to Rise – The Unspoken Principles Behind Power, Riches, and Lasting Wealth offers a reflective journey into the inner architecture of success, power, and fulfilment. It does not promise shortcuts, nor does it claim to possess absolute truths. Rather, it presents timeless principles, distilled through observation, introspection, and the lived experience of those who dared to rise—not only in the world, but within themselves.

The thoughts shared herein are designed to stir something deeper: a remembrance of your own power, a confrontation with your own beliefs, and an awakening to the clarity that already lives within you. This book is not a substitute for your own discernment, practical wisdom, or professional counsel in financial, psychological, or legal matters. The concepts within are not guarantees of wealth, but mirrors to help you examine how you define it, pursue it, and live with it.

Every individual's path is unique. What empowers one may challenge another. What elevates one person may humble the next. And this is the sacred nature of the journey—there are no universal formulas, only personal awakenings.

This book is meant to be held with presence. Question it. Wrestle with it. Let it speak to you not as doctrine, but as dialogue.

True power does not come from imitation, but from integration.

True wealth is not measured by accumulation, but by alignment.

And true success is not in reaching the top, but in remembering who you are as you rise.

Read with an open heart. Act with grounded wisdom. Rise with conscious intent.

Note - If any part of the book, in any sequence, hurts the reader's sentiments, it would be just out of a sheer accident not intentional

EPIGRAM

Born to Rise

"Where power meets peace, and wealth becomes wisdom."

– Shree Shambav

Born to Rise

The Unspoken Principles Behind Power, Riches, and Lasting Wealth

Shree Shambav

Shree Shambav is a 39x best-selling author renowned for his transformative works in personal development and spiritual growth.

Dear Cherished Readers

Dear Cherished Readers,

As I embark on this new literary voyage, my heart swells with profound gratitude and an overwhelming sense of connection. With deep emotion, I extend my heartfelt appreciation to each of you who has joined me on this journey.

With sincere warmth, I invite you to revisit the steps we have taken together through the pages of my earlier works. Our odyssey began with "Journey of Soul - Karma," a book that marked my first foray into the world of words and a testament to the raw passion that ignited my writing adventure.

The subsequent chapters of our shared journey unfolded through the enchanting tapestry of the *"Twenty + One"* series. With each page turned, it felt as though a brushstroke was added to the canvas of our collective imagination—stories and sentiments woven to echo within the quiet corners of your heart. These weren't just words; they were invitations to feel, to reflect, and to remember what truly matters.

And how can I not cherish the transformative path we walked together through the *"Life Changing Journey—Inspirational Quotes Series?"* Day by day, quote by quote, we ventured inward—into spaces often overlooked—to find wisdom in simplicity and light in life's shadows. Each reflection was offered as a gentle whisper of hope, a spark meant to uplift, inspire, and remind us that even in silence, the soul speaks.

The release of "Death - Light of Life and the Shadow of Death" promises to shed new light on the timeless mystery of death.

The **Optimum Python Series** is a comprehensive guide designed to empower readers at every stage of their programming journey. It begins with *Series I: Ultimate Guide for Beginners*, which lays a strong foundation in Python, making it accessible and engaging for newcomers. *Series II: Exploring Data Structures and Algorithms* takes the next step, offering a deep dive into core computer science principles that enhance problem-solving skills and coding efficiency. Building on this, *Series III: Python Power for Data Science* introduces powerful libraries such as NumPy, Pandas, Matplotlib, and Scikit-learn, guiding readers through data manipulation, visualisation, and foundational machine learning techniques. Finally, *Series IV: Unleashing the Potential of Data Science with Machine Learning Techniques* explores advanced machine learning models and real-world applications, enabling readers to harness the full potential of data-driven insights. Whether you're just starting out or looking to master sophisticated tools and strategies, this series is your roadmap to Python proficiency and beyond.

Shree Shambav expands his artistic repertoire with "*Whispers of Eternity: 150 Plus - A Symphony of Soulful Verses*," a heartfelt exploration of the human experience. Alongside this, his "*Whispers of the Soul: A Journey Through Haiku*" distils profound insights into poignant verses. Together, these works showcase his versatility and mastery of soulful expression, inviting readers on a journey of self-discovery. Through his poetry, he weaves a rich tapestry of emotion that resonates deeply with the heart.

Shree Shambav's latest works—*Learn to Love Yourself: A Journey of Discovering Inner Beauty and Strength Through 10 Transformative Rules, The Power of Letting Go: Embrace Freedom and Happiness, A Journey of Lasting Peace*—are true treasures of self-discovery, *The Entitlement Trap: Get Over It, Get On, Whispers of a Dying Soul: Unspoken Regrets and Unlived Dreams, Whispers of Silence - Unlocking Inner Power through Stillness, The Power of Words: Transforming Speech, Transforming Lives, The Art of Intentional Living: Minimalism for a Life of Purpose, Awakening the Infinite: The Power of Consciousness in Transforming Life, Beyond the Veil: A Journey Through Life After Death series, Bonds Beyond Blood - Where love builds bridges, and bonds defy blood., A Journey into Spiritual Maturity - 12 Golden Rules for Inner Transformation, The Seeker's Gold: Unlocking Life's Greatest Treasure and The Power of Manifestation - Unlocking The Path From Thought To Reality.*

In addition to these works, Shree Shambav has recently ventured into astrology with the release of *Astrology Unveiled – Foundations of Ancient Wisdom Series I to VI*, expanding into the realm of metaphysics. These books explore the foundational principles of Vedic astrology, offering readers a rich and practical understanding of this ancient wisdom.

Your unwavering support, enthusiasm to immerse yourself in my writings, and readiness to embark on these journeys with me have been my greatest sources of inspiration. Your input has been a beacon guiding me through the creation process, moulding these stories into containers of passion, emotion, knowledge, and resonance.

As I unveil this new narrative before you, know that your presence, insights, and shared moments have been my companions. The path we have walked together is etched in the annals of my creative evolution, and it's an honour beyond words to have you by my side once more.

Here's to the readers who have illuminated my path with their presence, who have embraced my stories with open hearts, and who have woven themselves into the very fabric of my literary world. Our journey has been a symbiotic dance of writer and reader, a harmony of souls brought together by the magic of storytelling.

With a heart brimming with appreciation and eyes glistening with anticipation, I extend my deepest gratitude for your unwavering support. Thank you for the memories, the shared emotions, and the countless hours spent in the worlds we've crafted together. As we step into this new adventure, let's continue to explore, feel, and discover the boundless horizons that words can unveil.

Warmly,

Shree Shambav

BORN TO RISE

Suggested Reads

FROM BEST-SELLING AUTHOR

Endorsements

"Raw, wise, and deeply empowering—Born to Rise is not just a book, it's a mirror and a map. Shree Shambav has masterfully unpacked the hidden layers of power, riches, and true wealth in a way that is both practical and profoundly spiritual. If you're tired of empty formulas and ready for a richer, more awakened life, this book is your next step. Prepare to be challenged, inspired, and forever changed."

— Rajini, Entrepreunuer

About the Author

Shree Shambav is an internationally acclaimed best-selling author, inspirational speaker, artist, philanthropist, life coach, strategist and entrepreneur. A world record holder, his deep passion for music led him to create soul-stirring albums, drawing inspiration from his celebrated poetry collection, Whispers of Eternity. His profound insights have sparked deep personal transformations, guiding countless individuals toward self-discovery, purposeful living, and authenticity.

With an extraordinary ability to unlock human potential, Shree empowers individuals to break through limitations and embrace their highest selves. His writings, lectures, and compassionate guidance continue to uplift lives, fostering resilience, mindfulness, and personal growth.

Shree Shambav is a 39x best-selling author celebrated for his profound contributions to personal development and spiritual growth.

Shree Shambav's literary journey took flight with the celebrated Journey of Soul - Karma, where he delved into the depths of human experience to unveil profound insights. Garnering recognition through multiple literature awards, his repertoire includes esteemed works, such as the Twenty + One Series, and the enlightening Life Changing Journey – Inspirational Quotes series.

As a distinguished alumnus of the Indian Institute of Management and the National Institute of Technology, Shree Shambav brings a wealth of corporate acumen from his tenure in multinational corporations. His most recent publications, including Unveiling the Enigma, Death - Light of Life and the Shadow of Death and Optimum – Power Python Series I, Series II, Series III and Series IV, demonstrate his mastery of both the literary and technical spheres.

Shree Shambav expands his artistic repertoire with "*Whispers of Eternity: 150 Plus - A Symphony of Soulful Verses*," a heartfelt exploration of the human experience. Alongside this, his "*Whispers of the Soul: A Journey Through Haiku*" distils profound insights into poignant verses. Together, these works showcase his versatility and mastery of soulful expression, inviting readers on a journey of self-discovery. Through his poetry, he weaves a rich tapestry of emotion that resonates deeply with the heart.

Shree Shambav's latest works—*Learn to Love Yourself: A Journey of Discovering Inner Beauty and Strength Through 10 Transformative*

Rules, The Power of Letting Go: Embrace Freedom and Happiness, A Journey of Lasting Peace—are true treasures of self-discovery, *The Entitlement Trap: Get Over It, Get On, Whispers of a Dying Soul: Unspoken Regrets and Unlived Dreams, Whispers of Silence - Unlocking Inner Power through Stillness, The Power of Words: Transforming Speech, Transforming Lives, The Art of Intentional Living: Minimalism for a Life of Purpose, Awakening the Infinite: The Power of Consciousness in Transforming Life, Beyond the Veil: A Journey Through Life After Death series, Bonds Beyond Blood - Where love builds bridges, and bonds defy blood., A Journey into Spiritual Maturity - 12 Golden Rules for Inner Transformation, The Seeker's Gold: Unlocking Life's Greatest Treasure* and *The Power of Manifestation - Unlocking The Path From Thought To Reality.*

In addition to these works, Shree Shambav has recently ventured into astrology with the release of Astrology Unveiled – Foundations of Ancient Wisdom Series I to VI, expanding into the realm of metaphysics. These books explore the foundational principles of Vedic astrology, offering readers a rich and practical understanding of this ancient wisdom.

Shree Shambav established the Ayur Rakshita Foundation, which is dedicated to promoting boundless growth, universal fraternity, and environmental protection. The charity helps diverse communities while working for societal progress.

To learn more about Shree Shambav and his works, visit his website at www.shambav.org. For information about the Ayur Rakshita Foundation and its initiatives, visit www.shambav-ayurrakshita.org.

Let's Follow him on Social Media: **@shreeshambav**

Main: https://linktr.ee/shreeshambav

SHREE SHAMBAV

Website: https://www.shambav.org/

LinkedIn: https://www.linkedin.com/in/shreeshambav/

Blog: https://blog.shambav.org/

Instagram: https://www.instagram.com/shreeshambav/

YouTube: https://www.youtube.com/@shreeshambav

Amazon: https://www.amazon.com/author/shreeshambav

Goodreads: https://www.goodreads.com/author/show/22367436.Shree_Shambav

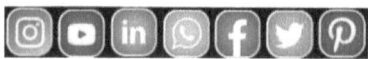

PREFACE

"True wealth begins when we stop chasing and start becoming."

- Shree Shambav

Born to Rise – The Unspoken Principles Behind Power, Riches, and Lasting Wealth

There comes a moment in every person's life when the quiet hum beneath the noise of daily existence grows louder—whispers that question, Is this all there is? Is there more to who I am and what I can become?

This book was born from that whisper.

Not from a desire to chase more, but from a deeper call to understand what more truly means.

Power. Riches. Wealth.

Three words that dominate ambitions, headlines, and dreams. But few ever pause to define them. Fewer still realise they are not the same. And almost no one tells you that the path to them—when walked unconsciously—can lead to emptiness instead of fulfilment.

This book is not about chasing illusions or glamorising success. It is about stripping these words down to their essence. It is about building a new language of achievement—one that rises from clarity, not confusion; from intention, not imitation.

You see, the world today sells a version of success that is loud, relentless, and outward. But true power is often quiet. Richness, subtle. And wealth—when real—is not just measured in numbers but in how those numbers reflect your values, time, freedom, and impact.

You were not born to fit into a system that measures worth by accumulation alone.

You were born to rise—to ascend with awareness, to wield influence with integrity, and to design a life that feels as good as it looks.

This first volume is your foundation.

It begins with clarity—defining what power, riches, and wealth truly mean in a world that distorts them. Then it moves into mindset—the inner landscape that either builds your rise or breaks it before it begins. We'll explore mental models, the art of strategic compounding, and the often misunderstood psychology of money. These are not just financial tools—they are philosophical tools. Tools that shape how you think, how you choose, and how you lead.

This book is not about giving you answers—it's about awakening the right questions.

It's not a ladder you climb. It's a lens you refine.

Because when you see clearly, you act powerfully. And when you act from power—true power—you don't just succeed. You rise.

Let this be your beginning—not just of wealth, but of wisdom. Not just of strategy, but of soul.

Turn the page. Your foundation awaits.

And beyond it, a life only you were born to build.

You were not born to merely survive.

You were born to rise.

Let the ascent begin.

With gratitude and encouragement,

Shree Shambav

INTRODUCTION

The Silent Forces That Shape Destiny

Every great rise begins in silence.

Not in applause, not in recognition, but in quiet moments of reckoning—where you confront the gap between who you are and who you were meant to become.

Most people spend their lives reacting to the world around them. They chase shadows of success, mimic the moves of others, and build lives that look good but feel hollow. Not because they lack ambition—but because they lack clarity. Clarity of what they truly seek. Clarity of what power, riches, and wealth actually mean—not just to society, but to them.

This book begins with a truth many overlook:

You are already powerful.

You are already rich in ways the world may never measure. And wealth is not something you chase—it is something you uncover and cultivate from within.

But here's the paradox—these truths remain dormant in most lives, buried beneath the noise of comparison, the fear of not-enough, and the conditioning that tells you to follow instead of forge.

This book is your map back to yourself.

It is not a manual of tactics—it is a journey through the inner architecture that governs your outer results. Because the world doesn't give you what you want. It mirrors who you are. And who you are is shaped by what you believe—about power, about money, about yourself.

So before we build, we must understand.

Before we ascend, we must unlearn.

And before we accumulate, we must align.

In Part I, we will redefine the very landscape you've been taught to navigate—exploring the deeper meanings of power, riches, and wealth. You'll learn why confusing these terms leads to inner conflict, and how clearly seeing their distinctions can liberate your choices.

In Part II, we move inward—to the mindset, psychology, and strategy of those who rise with purpose and stay rooted in fulfilment. This is where we talk about mental mastery, strategic compounding, the hidden emotions behind money, and the silent forces that either drive or derail your destiny.

This book does not promise overnight success.

What it offers is far more valuable: a **foundation**—timeless, internal, and unshakable.

Because power without clarity is dangerous.

Riches without wisdom are fleeting.

And wealth without meaning is just a prettier form of poverty.

You were born to rise.

Not merely to succeed, but to lead. Not merely to earn, but to embody.

And this is the first step—to remember who you are, and to reclaim the forces within you that shape your future long before the world sees your rise.

Let us begin—

Not with noise, but with knowing.

— Shree Shambav

A New Kind of Rich

Rich in spirit.

Rich in time.

Rich in impact.

Rich in peace.

This is the wealth the world forgets to talk about.

But it is the only kind that truly lasts.

If you feel the pull to live beyond the surface…

If you are tired of the illusions…

If you are ready to build something that the world cannot take from you…

Then this book is your companion.

It's time to rise—not just higher, but deeper.

To not just succeed, but **transcend**.

To not just make a living, but **craft a legacy**.

Welcome to *Born to Rise*.

Let's begin the ascent.

— **Shree Shambav**

PROLOGUE

Before the Rise

When the World Goes Quiet

There are moments in life that don't announce themselves.

Moments that arrive without noise or ceremony—yet mark the beginning of everything that follows.

For some, it is a quiet dissatisfaction in the middle of success.

For others, it is the sting of failure, a betrayal, a collapse, or simply a strange emptiness despite achieving all that was once dreamed.

We call it many names—midlife, awakening, breakdown, breakthrough.

But beneath the label lies one simple truth:

Something within you is done pretending.

Done pretending that success alone can fulfil you.
Done pretending that being busy means being important.
Done pretending that following the rules will lead to freedom.

In that silence—raw and unfiltered—you begin to see with new eyes.

You begin to ask the deeper questions:

What am I really building?

Whose definition of power am I chasing?

Is this wealth… or just a collection of well-decorated fears?

This book was born from that silence.

Not the kind found in isolation, but the kind that follows awakening.

You see, the world will teach you to run—faster, harder, louder.

It rarely teaches you how to rise—with intention, alignment, and inner clarity.

It celebrates those who "make it," but forgets to ask: Make it to what? And at what cost?

So before we chase another goal, we must pause.

Before we climb higher, we must ask: Is the ladder leaning on the right wall?

Because power, when misunderstood, becomes control.

Riches, when untethered from purpose, become anxiety.

And wealth, without inner clarity, becomes a golden cage—impressive from the outside, but hollow within.

But power, when rooted in purpose, becomes presence.

Riches, when guided by meaning, become impact.

And wealth, when aligned with the soul, becomes legacy.

This book is your invitation to that deeper path.

Not a rejection of material mastery, but a redefinition of it.

Not a denial of ambition, but a refinement of it.

Not an escape from the world, but a return to your truest self within it.

Here, you will find the foundations of a new way to rise— A way where clarity is the compass, mindset is the engine, and fulfilment is not postponed until the end, but woven into every step of the journey.

So let this be the moment where the world goes quiet… And something eternal within you begins to speak.

You were not just born to survive.

Not just born to succeed.

You were born to rise.

And the time has come.

— Shree Shambav

CONTENTS

DEDICATION iii
DISCLAIMER v
EPIGRAM vii
Dear Cherished Readers xi
Suggested Reads xv
Endorsements xvii
About the Author xix
PREFACE xxiii
INTRODUCTION xxvii
A New Kind of Rich xxxi
PROLOGUE xxxiii
CONTENTS xxxvii
Introduction 1
   The Silent Forces That Shape Destiny 1
PART ONE 1
   CLARITY — Understanding the Landscape 1
CHAPTER I 1
   What Is Power? 1
CHAPTER II 17
   What Is Rich? 17
CHAPTER III 37

- What Is Wealth? 37

CHAPTER IV 59
- Rich vs. Wealthy vs. Powerful 59

PART TWO 77
- MINDSET - Shaping the Inner World 77

CHAPTER V 79
- The Mind Behind the Rise 79

CHAPTER VI 99
- Strategies of the Powerful and Wealthy 99

CHAPTER VII 123
- The Art of Compounding Everything 123

CHAPTER VIII 151
- The Psychology of Money 151

WRAP UP 177
- The Sacred Pause 177

BRIDGE 195
- From Ambition to Alignment 195

Life Coach and Philanthropist 201

TESTIMONIALS 203

ACKNOWLEDGEMENTS 211

Introduction

The Silent Forces That Shape Destiny

"The climb from survival to self-mastery begins the moment you stop reacting and start remembering who you are."

- Shree Shambav

Synopsis:

The Silent Forces That Shape Destiny

This introduction sets the philosophical and emotional foundation for the book. It challenges traditional notions of success by revealing the unseen energies, mental programs, and spiritual truths that determine who truly rises in life—not just financially, but in awareness and impact. Divided into three key parts, this chapter explores myths around money and power, redefines wealth through the lens of consciousness, and invites the reader to rise beyond survival into intentional self-mastery. It's not merely about gaining more, but becoming more.

If you stay there any longer."

The Mirage of the Mountain: Myths That Mislead the Climb

In a small village nestled beneath a towering mountain, lived a boy named Arup who spent his days staring up at the distant peak. The elders spoke in hushed tones of those who had reached the summit—how they returned wrapped in gold, cloaked in influence, and seemingly untouched by sorrow. To young Arup, the mountain became a metaphor for success, and the stories became his blueprint.

He set out, as many do, chasing **power**, **riches**, and **wealth**, believing them to be destinations. But like many in our modern world, Arup climbed not with clarity, but with cultural myths strapped tightly to his back. Myths are so deeply woven into our societal fabric that they shape our ambitions long before we question their truth.

Myth 1: Power is Domination

"If I am powerful, I can control outcomes. People will listen. I will never be hurt again."

This is perhaps the oldest illusion—that power is loud, external, and forceful. We are conditioned to believe that power is dominance, command over others, or the ability to influence through fear or status. But this myth distorts our inner compass.

True power is not what bends others, but what holds you steady in the storm. It is the calm centre in a world of chaos. It is found in restraint, not aggression; in presence, not performance.

Arup once entered a boardroom with a rehearsed voice and an iron will. He left, silenced by a woman who spoke softly—but every word struck truth like lightning. Her power wasn't volume—it was **clarity**, born from inner alignment.

Myth Busted: *Power isn't about controlling others—it's about not being controlled by your own fears.*

Myth 2: Riches Are the Goal

"If I get rich, I'll be free. Life will finally begin."

The image is seductive: luxury cars, penthouses, designer lives. We're taught that riches are the doorway to joy, yet so many walk through that door only to find an echoing emptiness on the other side. Why? Because riches are often measured externally—income, assets, visibility—not by internal peace or freedom.

Arup built a tech empire by thirty. The world clapped. But every night, he lay awake, anxious, isolated, overworked. His riches had bought more walls, not more freedom. He had gained everything the world promised—and lost what mattered most: peace of mind.

Myth Busted: *Riches are not the goal—they are a tool. When misused, they build cages instead of wings.*

Myth 3: Wealth Is Only Financial

"If I accumulate enough money, I'll be wealthy."

This myth reduces wealth to digits in a bank account. But real wealth is multidimensional. It is time with your children. It is your ability to say "no" to what drains your soul. It is health, vitality, emotional richness, intellectual capital, spiritual calm, and the relationships that ground and elevate you.

Arup eventually met a monk by the river—one who had no possessions, yet radiated serenity. The monk said, "The wealthiest man I knew died with a full bank and an empty heart. You don't want that kind of inheritance."

Myth Busted: *Wealth isn't what you keep—it's what continues to grow inside you, even if everything external is stripped away.*

The Deeper Distortion: Surface Success vs. Soul Fulfilment

These myths aren't just innocent misunderstandings—they're **systemic seductions**. They lure us into chasing shadows while neglecting our essence. Schools teach careers, not purpose. Media showcases status, not substance. Culture elevates busyness, not balance.

We end up like Arup—chasing summit after summit, only to realise the peak was never the point. **The real treasure was learning who we became along the way**, and what parts of ourselves we had to reclaim to feel whole.

A New Compass

To rise consciously, we must rewrite the story:

- Power is presence.
- Riches are tools.

- Wealth is harmony.

The modern seeker must become a **weaver**—threading inner values with outer pursuits, using discernment as a compass and authenticity as a map.

The world doesn't need more people chasing false summits. It needs more awakened climbers—those who know that the real ascent begins the moment you question the mountain itself.

The Currency of Consciousness: Arup's Journey Beyond Success

Arup was always brilliant. From a young age, he stood out—not just for his intellect, but for his relentless drive. By thirty-two, he had the accolades many spend a lifetime chasing: a corner office, luxury cars, global recognition, and a digital following in the millions. To the world, Arup had arrived. But in the quiet hours, long after the applause faded, he felt strangely hollow.

It was a peculiar emptiness—one that success couldn't fill, one that applause couldn't silence.

He began to ask questions he had once dismissed as indulgent: *Why do I still feel incomplete? Is this all there is? Who am I beyond these titles?*

That's when his real journey began—not toward another external peak, but inward.

An Unexpected Encounter

In a remote mountain village in Himachal, where Arup had retreated for solitude, he met an old woman named **Savitri Amma**. She lived in a small stone house, wore no watch, and didn't own a phone. Yet people travelled miles to speak with her. Her presence alone was magnetic—quiet, grounded, profoundly awake.

One evening, as they sat by a slow-burning fire under a moonlit sky, Arup asked, "How do you know so much about life when you've had so little?"

She smiled gently and replied,

"You think I've had little because you're counting in rupees and likes. I've spent my life in attention, in stillness. I've invested not in what I own, but how deeply I can see."

That night, Arup couldn't sleep. He realised he had been trading his life for a currency that depreciated quickly: trends, metrics, validations. But Amma operated on a different currency altogether—**consciousness**.

Consciousness as Currency

What does it mean?

Consciousness is awareness sharpened by stillness, intention purified by alignment, and presence deepened by truth. While money buys things, consciousness shapes moments. While fame may fill rooms, consciousness fills lives.

Arup saw this clearly. The leaders he admired not just for their achievements but their essence—those who left behind not just empires but echoes of meaning—were people of extraordinary consciousness.

- Their decisions were not reactions, but reflections.
- Their wealth was not just accumulated, but emanated.
- Their influence was not loud, but lasting.

They operated from clarity, not chaos. From wisdom, not worry. From depth, not desperation.

From Transaction to Transformation

Arup began to reorient his life. He still ran companies and made investments, but now **conscious intention became the filter**. He no longer did things to prove. He acted to express, to serve, to align.

Whereas before he used to ask, *What's the ROI?*, now he asked,

Does this bring peace, growth, truth?

Will this deepen or dilute my presence?

That one shift changed everything. Deals came more easily. Relationships grew richer. His days felt fuller—not with tasks, but with meaning. He began teaching others not just how to succeed, but how to awaken. Because **a life lived unconsciously, no matter how rich, is bankrupt in spirit.**

Legacy, Rewritten

Years later, Arup would be remembered not just as a titan of industry but as a torchbearer of a deeper way of living. His legacy wasn't the company he built, but the consciousness he awakened in others. He hadn't just succeeded—he had transformed. And in doing so, he left behind something wealthier than riches: a ripple of inner revolution.

In the end, consciousness is the only currency accepted across all dimensions of life—relationships, decisions, time, and even death. When we cultivate it, we begin to transact in truth. When we embody it, we become instruments of legacy.

From Chasing to Rising: Arup's Ascent into Self-Mastery

Arup's job was not glamorous. It was survival. Long nights, relentless targets. He didn't sleep much. His meals were timed by urgency, not hunger. His worth—self-measured through promotions and praise—became tethered to how much he could endure.

Every morning felt like war. Not just against competition, but against time, bills, and self-doubt. He called it a hustle. Others called it ambition. But deep down, it was **fear wearing a suit**—fear of being left behind, of being unseen, of never being enough.

He was surviving.

Until the crash came—not a financial one, but an emotional collapse. Arup found himself in a hospital bed, his body refusing to cooperate. Burnout, said the doctors. Breakdown, whispered his own soul.

The Illusion of Constant Climbing

In the hospital's sterile silence, he confronted a haunting question:

What have I been running from? And what have I been running toward?

He realised he had been **climbing a mountain someone else told him to climb**, convinced that at the peak there would be peace. But there was no summit, only exhaustion.

This is the nature of the **survival mindset**—it keeps us chasing approval, hoarding safety, and avoiding shame. It builds careers that drain, relationships that feel transactional, and inner voices that constantly scream, *"Not yet. Not enough."*

Survival makes us reactive. It trades vision for vigilance. It teaches us to adapt, but not to **transform**.

The First Step Inward

Arup began the slow journey back. But this time, not outward—**inward**.

He took long walks with no destination. He studied wisdom traditions. He journaled not for answers, but for honesty. He meditated—not to escape—but to return.

And most importantly, he listened. To the part of him that had been silenced under layers of performance.

This was the beginning of **self-mastery**—not in controlling the world, but in understanding his own inner weather. He began observing his fears instead of obeying them. He replaced compulsive doing with conscious being. He saw how his survival mind made every opportunity a threat, every silence a danger, every rest a weakness.

Self-mastery was not about becoming perfect. It was about becoming whole.

From Outer Noise to Inner Compass

Imagine two ships in the ocean.

One is tossed by every wave, reacting to wind, constantly recalculating its course in panic. That's the survival mind.

The other—its anchor is deep. Its direction is guided by stars, not storms. That's self-mastery.

Arup's life changed not because the world changed—but because his relationship with the world transformed. He no longer made decisions from fear of missing out, but from fullness within. He no longer spoke to impress, but to express. He no longer hustled to be worthy, but acted from worthiness.

And something extraordinary happened:

- People began to listen when he spoke, not because he was loud, but because he was present.

- Influence flowed to him, not because he demanded it, but because he embodied it.

- His success expanded—not in frantic leaps, but in graceful alignment.

Impact That Echoes

The old Arup built empires that looked impressive. The new Arup built movements that felt true.

He mentored young leaders—not just in scaling business, but in grounding identity. He taught them that the most powerful people are not those who conquer markets, but those who have mastered themselves.

Because when we operate from self-mastery:

- We lead from clarity, not compulsion.
- We give from overflow, not obligation.
- We create not to prove, but to serve.

This shift is not a tweak. It is a **transformation**.

From Striving to Becoming

To live in survival is to live as a **shadow** of your own possibility.
To rise into self-mastery is to become **a conscious architect of your destiny**.

And Arup's life?

It became not just a story of success, but a transmission of awakening.

Closing Reflection

We don't rise by adding more to the outside. We rise when we remove what silences the inside.

Survival builds walls.

Self-mastery builds presence.

And when one person makes that leap—from chasing to becoming—they don't just change their life. They alter the frequency of everyone they touch.

Imagine two seeds planted in the same soil. Given the same sunlight, the same water, the same environment. One grows into a towering tree. The other barely breaks the surface. From the outside, it might seem like fate or chance. But underneath—quite literally—something deeper is happening.

This is the unseen story of countless lives. Two people start from similar places. One breaks generational curses and rises into power, influence, and peace. The other cycles through struggle, never quite escaping scarcity. Why?

It is because the soil of circumstance is only one part of growth. What truly determines whether someone rises or remains stuck is the root system—the inner world of beliefs, alignment, energy, and purpose. These are the **silent forces** that shape destiny.

Arup's Story: The Invisible Cage

Arup grew up in a modest village where hard work was religion and ambition was often considered arrogance. His father, a tailor, believed deeply in honesty and effort—but also carried a quiet bitterness. "People like us," he would say, "are not meant to rise too high. That's for others."

Arup never questioned it until the day he met Kalyani—a woman who had once lived in the same village, but now returned with an aura of peace and abundance. She hadn't inherited wealth. She had built it. But not just materially—she radiated something different. A kind of *inner spaciousness*, a clarity that made even silence feel rich.

Over tea beneath the banyan tree, Arup asked her how she did it.

She smiled, "I changed my relationship with who I thought I was. I stopped believing I was born to survive—and started acting like I was born to lead."

The Hidden Patterns

Here's what Kalyani meant—and what so many never learn:

1. Mindset is the first architect of reality.

People who rise don't merely "hope" for success. They *expect* it—not with arrogance, but with alignment. Their inner dialogue is not one of fear, but faith. Not empty positivity, but rooted clarity. They've learned to think like creators, not victims of circumstance.

2. Belief is the blueprint.

What you believe about money, self-worth, relationships, and power silently governs every choice. Those who rise question about inherited beliefs. They examine every thought and ask: *Is this mine, or something I was taught by someone still stuck?*

3. Energetic alignment is real.

We all emit a frequency—through our thoughts, emotions, and presence. People stuck in cycles of lack often carry energies of desperation, comparison, or self-doubt. Those who rise move in peace, clarity, and service. The world responds differently to each frequency.

4. Purpose transforms pain into power.

Everyone experiences setbacks. But those who rise *assign meaning* to their suffering. They don't just ask, "Why me?" They ask, "How can this be used for good?" Their purpose becomes fuel. Their pain becomes their platform.

The River and the Dam

Think of life like a river. The water wants to flow. That flow is your natural rise—towards growth, abundance, and contribution. But somewhere along the path, dams get built. These are beliefs like:

- "I'm not good enough."
- "People like me don't succeed."
- "If I shine, I'll be judged."

These dams are invisible to the outside world. But they block the flow. And unless they're consciously dismantled, no amount of effort can create a breakthrough.

Those who rise do inner excavation. They clear the dams. And suddenly, the river flows again—not through struggle, but surrender.

Success is not random. It's not reserved for the lucky. It's coded in the silent agreements we've made with life—many of which we never chose. The question is: are you willing to rewrite those agreements?

Because once you do, you'll discover what Arup did that day under the banyan tree—that rising isn't about becoming someone else. It's about remembering who you were before the world told you to settle.

PART ONE

CLARITY — Understanding the Landscape

"Hard power may silence voices, but only soft power inspires hearts."

- *Shree Shambav*

CHAPTER I

What Is Power?

"The most unshakable power is the one that doesn't need to be announced—it's felt."

- Shree Shambav

Synopsis:

This foundational chapter unpacks the layered and often misunderstood concept of power. It begins by redefining power not as domination or status—but as the subtle art of influence, self-command, and energetic presence. Through the distinctions between hard vs. soft power and earned vs. imposed power, readers are guided to see how real power doesn't come from force but from alignment, clarity, and deep internal grounding. Power is not what you hold over others—it's what you hold within yourself. This chapter lays the groundwork for building a legacy rooted in strength, not control.

Power. It's one of the most misunderstood forces in the world. We see it on stages and screens—loud, commanding, dressed in suits, driving sleek cars, issuing orders. But what if that isn't power at all?

What if true power is quiet?

What if it doesn't raise its voice, but deepens its presence?

What if it lives not in dominance over others, but in deep dominion over oneself?

The Story of Arup: The Two Thrones

Arup once believed power meant having the final word.

Raised in a world where success was measured by control—over time, people, and outcomes—he pursued influence with intensity. Titles, trophies, and approval became his compass. He could negotiate deals, manage teams, and silence criticism. But behind closed doors, Arup felt hollow. Exhausted. Performative.

His life was impressive from the outside, yet inside, he was constantly battling anxiety, insecurity, and a haunting emptiness.

Until one day, he met someone who changed everything—a quiet, unassuming man named Raghavan. No fame. No following. Just presence. When Raghavan walked into a room, it calmed. When he spoke, even silence leaned in to listen. He wasn't loud. He wasn't in charge. Yet people turned to him in crisis. Trusted him in chaos.

Arup once asked him, "How do you command so much respect… without ever asking for it?"

Raghavan simply said, "There's a difference between sitting on a throne made of gold, and sitting on the throne of your own soul."

Inner Strength vs. External Control

Let's draw the distinction clearly.

1. External control is rooted in fear.

It says: "If I don't control everything, I will lose everything."

It's reactive. It tightens. It manipulates. It requires constant performance.

This kind of power is brittle. One challenge, one rejection, and it crumbles. It seeks validation from the outside, always hungry, always insecure.

2. Inner strength is rooted in trust.

It whispers: "No matter what happens out there, I remain whole in here."

It's grounded. It responds, rather than reacts. It's driven by intention, not ego.

This kind of power is fluid. Resilient. It doesn't need to prove—it *moves*. It doesn't need followers to feel worthy. Its confidence is born from alignment, not applause.

The Tree and the Tent

Imagine two structures: a massive tent and a deeply rooted tree.

The tent looks big. It's expansive, flashy. But if the wind changes, it collapses. It needs constant support, constant maintenance.

The tree, though… it grows slow. Quiet. But its roots go deep. It sways, but it doesn't fall. It weathers storms because its power is embedded in its being, not in how tall it appears.

External control is the tent. Inner strength is the tree.

Power that Lasts

The world often rewards performers. But legacy belongs to those with inner sovereignty.

You see it in Gandhi's silence, in Mandela's forgiveness, in a mother's quiet courage, in a healer's presence, in an artist's truth. They don't control the world—they transform it, because they've already transformed themselves.

That's the heart of real power: Not in how many people you can lead, but in how well you can lead yourself.

Not in how many rules you write, but in how many wounds you've alchemised.

Not in how high you rise—but how deeply you've rooted.

The Shift That Changes Everything

When Arup finally let go of his obsession with image, and began the slow, sacred journey inward, everything changed. He no longer chased influence—he *became* influential. Not because he fought for attention, but because his presence began to carry weight. Stillness. Clarity. Compassion.

And in that space, he discovered:

Power is not something you wield. It's something you embody.

Imagine two rivers flowing side by side.

One crashes with force—carving cliffs, breaking boulders, making itself known with thunderous might. The other flows gently—patient, persistent, shaping the landscape not through destruction but through quiet devotion over time.

These are the rivers of **hard power** and **soft power**.

And in today's world of leadership, influence, and legacy, both have their place—but only one endures.

The Two Kingdoms

There was once a land divided into two realms.

To the north ruled King Darvesh—strong, strategic, feared. His kingdom was built on rules, systems, and results. He believed in discipline, authority, and clear command. "Respect is earned through strength," he often said. And indeed, his kingdom thrived on order. Roads were clean. Taxes were paid. Structures stood tall.

To the south lived Queen Mira—wise, warm, deeply trusted. She ruled not by force, but by listening. Her kingdom wasn't known for its armies but for its art, its music, and its people who stayed not because they had to, but because they *wanted* to. She believed, "Influence is love wearing the cloak of wisdom."

Years passed. Storms came. Empires shook.

And when the dust settled, Darvesh's walls remained—but his people had quietly left. Mira's people, however, rebuilt what was lost, because they *believed* in her vision.

This is the truth: **Hard power builds empires. Soft power births civilisations.**

Defining the Two

Hard Power

- Based on control, authority, force, or tangible leverage.
- Seen in politics through military strength or economic sanctions.
- In business, it's seen in hierarchical control, decisions by title, and structural dominance.
- In relationships, it's about setting terms, enforcing boundaries with consequences.

It's necessary in moments of chaos, crisis, or when firm direction is needed. It establishes stability.

Soft Power

- Based on influence, inspiration, attraction, and emotional intelligence.
- In politics, it's diplomacy, cultural exchange, and shared values.
- In business, it's brand affinity, leadership charisma, storytelling, and emotional resonance.

- In relationships, it's trust, empathy, presence, and mutual growth.

It's invisible, but magnetic. Slow, but sustainable. It doesn't demand—it invites.

The Hammer and the Flame

A hammer can force things into place. Build quickly. Fix errors. But a flame? It warms. It melts resistance. It creates space for transformation, not just correction.

Hard power is the hammer. Necessary. Decisive. Sharp.

Soft power is the flame. Subtle. Transformative. Enduring.

Leadership Today: The Integration

Modern leadership isn't about choosing between hard or soft power—it's about knowing *when* and *how* to use both.

- In business, the CEO who can *command performance* while *inspiring belief* in a vision is unstoppable.

- In politics, the leader who protects a nation's interests while building bridges with compassion wins the long game.

- In personal growth, the one who disciplines their habits while nourishing their soul becomes unshakable.

- In relationships, those who set clear boundaries *and* hold space for healing create deeper bonds.

Hard power earns compliance. Soft power earns commitment.

Legacy: What Remains When You're Gone

Arup, in his younger years, used hard power to climb fast. He managed people. He closed deals. He won debates.

But it was only when he began listening deeply, understanding unspoken needs, and leading with intention rather than assertion, that his real legacy began to unfold.

It wasn't in the projects he built—but in the people he helped rise.

True legacy is not what you control while alive, but what continues to grow long after you're gone.

The Wisdom of Integration

You may need the sword. But wield it with a sage's grace.

You may possess fire. But use it to light the path, not scorch the earth.

You may command respect. But remember—hearts cannot be conquered, only earned.

What Makes Power Truly Earned, and Why Imposed Power Eventually Collapses

The Tale of the Twin Mountain

In a quiet valley nestled between two ancient mountains, two leaders once ruled neighbouring villages—Rajan and Arun.

Rajan, ambitious and admired, built fast. His voice was loud, his decisions final. He controlled his people with policies, punishments, and promises. Every home bore his symbol. Every mouth spoke his name. "Order," he said, "is the foundation of greatness."

Arun, quieter by nature, moved slowly. He listened more than he spoke. Instead of issuing commands, he asked questions. He shared stories around fires, broke bread with his people, and planted seeds—not just in soil, but in minds. "Trust," he believed, "is the soil where real power grows."

Years passed. Rajan's village grew into a fortress. Tall, intimidating. But behind the walls, fear festered. People obeyed, but love disappeared. Hearts went quiet.

Arun's village, though slower to build, became a tapestry of culture, kindness, and resilience. Decisions were shared. Mistakes were forgiven. Purpose, not punishment, shaped the collective will.

Then came the drought.

Water dried. Crops failed. Desperation spread.

In Rajan's kingdom, revolt came swiftly. The people, having been silenced too long, no longer feared losing what little they had. His power—once feared—shattered under the weight of unspoken resentment.

But in Arun's village, people came together. They remembered the wisdom Arun had nurtured. They shared, innovated, and adapted. The village didn't just survive—it grew stronger.

The Difference Between Imposed and Earned Power

Power imposed is like a **house built on glass**—it may shimmer and rise fast, but it fractures with the slightest tremor.

Power earned is like a **tree rooted deep**—it weathers storms, grows slowly, and offers shade long after the planter is gone.

Why Does Imposed Power Collapses?

1. **Fear Creates Distance**

Imposed power relies on fear, control, and performance. While it can create short-term obedience, it lacks emotional buy-in. People may comply—but they disconnect. The result is hollow allegiance.

2. **It Ignores Truth**

Imposed power resists feedback, vulnerability, and evolution. It defends its own illusion of strength. But power that denies truth eventually becomes brittle—one honest wind, and it breaks.

3. **It Consumes Itself**

Like a fire with no oxygen, dominance without trust burns fast and dies quickly. The energy it takes to maintain force is unsustainable. Without renewal through love, loyalty, or shared vision, it cannibalises itself.

What Makes Power Truly Earned

- **Sustainability through Trust**

Earned power is slower but lasting. It is *chosen* by others, not imposed upon them. It doesn't need to be defended—it is *invited*, *respected*, and *remembered*.

- **Built on Contribution, Not Control**

True power comes from how much one gives, not just what one commands. It's cultivated through service, integrity, and emotional presence.

- **Aligned with Truth, Not Ego**

Earned power allows truth to enter the room—even if it challenges the leader. This openness creates cultures of innovation, safety, and inner strength.

The Candle vs. the Flashlight

A flashlight shines directly. Bright, focused, forceful. But when batteries die, it's over.

A candle glows softly. It spreads warmth. And when another needs light—it shares its flame without losing its own.

Rajan was the flashlight. Arun, the candle.

And in the end, **the flame outlasted the force**.

The Legacy of Earned Power

Arun never needed his name etched into stone. He didn't seek worship—only wisdom, woven through generations.

His legacy was not in monuments, but in mindsets. Not in domination, but in devotion.

Because power rooted in alignment—with truth, with people, with purpose—doesn't end when the leader leaves. It expands.

So ask not: "How do I gain power?"

Ask instead:

"How do I become someone others rise around?"

"How do I hold truth, serve quietly, and light the way?"

That's the power that echoes across time.

From Control to Command: The Journey to Inner Authority

The Puppet and the Flame

There once lived a boy named Jhon in a bustling city of glowing screens, ticking clocks, and never-ending expectations. From a young age, his path was paved not by his own feet, but by invisible strings—expectations of family, metrics of success, roles to play. School taught him to conform. Society taught him to compare. And work taught him to compete. The world applauded him only when he obeyed it.

He was like a puppet in a grand theatre—perfect posture, rehearsed lines, painted smile. But inside, something flickered. A tiny flame that whispered, *"This is not all you are."*

That flame was his **inner authority**, waiting patiently beneath the noise.

The Nature of External Systems of Power

External systems of power—be they cultural norms, political structures, social status, or corporate ladders—are often built to **extract compliance**, not cultivate consciousness. They reward performance over presence, productivity over peace. And over time, we mistake these systems as the source of our worth.

We dress our wounds in gold. We silence our souls with applause.

But here's the truth: **Power that is borrowed is always brittle.**

When our sense of direction depends on validation, we lose our compass. When our choices are governed by fear of rejection, we live as guests in our own lives.

Jhon's Awakening

It wasn't a grand moment that changed Jhon. It was a quiet evening.

He sat at his desk, surrounded by awards he didn't remember earning, inboxes filled with demands, and a calendar that left no space for breath.

He looked in the mirror—and for the first time, **he didn't recognise the man staring back.**

Tired eyes. A fake smile. A heart filled with noise.

He whispered to himself, *"Whose life am I living?"*

In that moment, something cracked. And from the crack, light poured in.

The Shift: From External Control to Inner Sovereignty

This transformation isn't a single leap. It's a pilgrimage. Here are the sacred thresholds:

1. From Imitation to Intuition

When Jhon stopped chasing others' definitions of success, he began *hearing* himself. He spent time in stillness. He asked deeper questions. Not "What should I do?" but "What am I here to become?"

This is the shift from imitation to intuition. From following others' maps to writing your own legend.

2. From Reaction to Response

External systems train us to react—to emails, trends, and emergencies. Inner authority allows us to **respond**—with clarity, calm, and conscience.

Jhon began waking earlier. Not for work, but for presence.

Meditation. Movement. Reflection.

Not to escape the world, but to enter it **on his own terms**.

He stopped being pulled, and started **choosing**.

3. From Obedience to Integrity

He stopped saying "yes" when his soul said "no."

He walked away from projects that paid well but cost too much peace.

He learned that **inner peace is more profitable than outer approval.**

The Kite and the Wind

Most people live like kites in the sky—rising only as long as someone holds their string.

Their flight depends on conditions, control, and someone else's permission.

But Jhon discovered he was never the kite.

He was the **wind.**

The power was not in being held up.

The power was in knowing **he could rise from within.**

What Inner Authority Truly Means

Inner authority is **not rebellion.**

It's not arrogance or isolation.

Its sovereignty is rooted in **alignment**—between your values, voice, and vision.

It means you can sit at any table without needing to belong.

It means you can walk away, not from a place of pride—but from a place of power.

It's choosing silence over shouting.

It's owning your "no" as much as your "yes."

It's trusting that your truth, lived fully, is the most potent force you will ever wield.

Jhon Today

He still lives in the same city. Still navigates systems. But the difference?

He is no longer **owned** by them.

He no longer trades authenticity for applause.

He is a man lit from within—governed by something deeper than goals: **his soul's compass.**

He's not louder now.

Just **unshakably clear.**

And that clarity?

It moves mountains.

In a world that trains you to seek power outside yourself, the greatest revolution is to reclaim your own.

CHAPTER II

What Is Rich?

"Looking rich is easy. Living rich—with peace, purpose, and freedom—is rare."

– Shree Shambav

Synopsis

What Is Rich? Challenges the reader to go beneath the shiny surface of luxury and income brackets. It delves into the difference between appearing rich and feeling truly fulfilled. While material abundance and lifestyle markers often shape public perception, this section reveals how such indicators can be hollow if not rooted in purpose and inner peace. Richness is redefined through the lenses of time, freedom, and access—urging the reader to consider what they own that can't be bought. Ultimately, it invites a richer life by asking better questions about what truly matters.

The Mirage of More: Redefining "Rich"

The Gilded Mask

Arup stood at the edge of a penthouse balcony, champagne in hand, city lights flickering beneath him like a million desperate wishes. The room behind him buzzed with curated laughter, designer suits, and well-practised charm. He had made it—by every metric the world celebrates.

His startup had just sold. His face had appeared in magazines. His inbox overflowed with invitations, and his bank account, for the first time, echoed with the silence of "enough."

And yet, he felt hollow.

Not lost. Just… unanchored.

It was a strange feeling—to have arrived, and not feel at home.

The World's Definition of Rich

Society teaches us early what "rich" means:

- **Big house. Big car. Bigger titles.**
- **Luxury holidays. Designer clothes.**
- **Fame. Influence. Control.**

It's not just marketing. It's messaging.

From childhood, we're told that the ones who "have it all" are the ones who *own* the most.

But what is the cost of chasing that version of richness?

We begin to **measure our worth with numbers,**

compare our joy with appearances,

and trade our authenticity for applause.

We don't ask, *"Am I fulfilled?"*

We ask, *"Am I ahead?"*

The Story of Two Rich Men

Let me tell you about two men who lived in the same city as Arup.

Rohan had three homes, a fleet of luxury cars, and a portfolio that could buy silence in any room. But he also had insomnia. Paranoia. And relationships that revolved around his wallet, not his heart. He was rich. But not **whole**.

Sanjay, on the other hand, lived in a modest home, grew his own vegetables, mentored local youth, and woke every morning without an alarm clock. He never felt the need to impress—only to express. He didn't own much, but he felt **full**.

Which of them was rich?

The world would pick Rohan.

But the soul? It would choose Sanjay.

The Hidden Poverty in Abundance

Arup began to notice a pattern: many people he admired outwardly were inwardly exhausted. They were rich in **resources**, but poor in **resonance**.

They had mastered acquisition, but forgotten **appreciation**.

They had gathered followers, but lost **themselves**.

They were celebrated on social media but **wept in private**.

And slowly, Arup began to ask the question that changed everything:

"What if being rich isn't about what I have, but what I no longer need?"

The Mansion Without Windows

Chasing society's version of success is like building a massive mansion—one that touches the clouds—but forgetting to put in windows.

Yes, it looks magnificent from the outside.

But inside, it's dark. Cold. Airless.

The views may be spectacular, but if you can't breathe, what's the point?

The soul suffocates when success becomes a performance.

The Real Currency of Richness

Through this questioning, Arup found new forms of wealth:

- **Time to think deeply.**
- **Freedom to say no.**
- **Relationships where he could be real.**
- **Peace that wasn't rented by vacation.**
- **A life that wasn't dependent on applause to feel meaningful.**

He still earned. Still built. But now with **intention**, not insecurity.

He no longer wanted to be rich in lifestyle. He wanted to be rich in **life**.

Redefining Rich

To be truly rich means:

- To **wake up without dread**.
- To live in a way where your **values guide your choices**, not your fears.
- To be **remembered for your impact**, not just your image.
- To be able to give generously, not just from your surplus, but from your **presence**.

Arup found that once he changed his definition of rich, **everything else changed with it**. He wasn't chasing anymore. He was creating. Not performing—but becoming.

And in that shift, he found not just wealth—but **worth**.

Because the most dangerous poverty is the kind that wears a rich man's smile.

And the truest richness is the kind no one can see, but everyone can feel.

The Velvet Cage: When Illusions Cost More Than Poverty

The Illusion That Shouts, The Poverty That Whispers

Arup once met a man named Viren at a global entrepreneur summit in Singapore. Viren was polished, charismatic, and cloaked in luxury—Italian suits, rare watches, and a Rolex-like confidence that made heads turn.

Everyone admired him. Envied him, even.

But over a quiet rooftop conversation later that night, Arup saw something that didn't match the brand.

A flicker of exhaustion behind the eyes.

A silence between the sentences.

A sigh that betrayed the curated smile.

And then Viren said something that stayed with Arup for years:

"I'm not rich, brother. I just can't afford for anyone to think I'm not."

The Invisible Debt of Pretending

This is the hidden danger of **performative wealth**—the kind that must be constantly **maintained**, like a mask glued to the skin. The kind that doesn't come from abundance, but from **the fear of being seen without it.**

It's not material poverty that drains the soul.

It's the emotional **debt** of pretending.

Many people are bankrupt not in their bank accounts, but in their **spirit**:

- Bankrupt in **sleep**, because anxiety doesn't let them rest.
- Bankrupt in **authentic connection**, because every relationship is a transaction.
- Bankrupt in **peace**, because they're always racing to stay ahead of the image they've built.

They are rich in lifestyle, yet poor in **life**.

The Velvet Cage

Imagine a bird in a gilded cage.

The cage is lined with velvet. There's food, filtered water, mirrors, music, and praise from all who pass by.

But the bird cannot fly.

Its wings are clipped—not by force, but by **expectation**.

This is what the illusion of being rich does to people.

It offers the comfort of appearance while stealing the freedom of **truth**.

It celebrates the packaging and ignores the **emptiness inside**.

True poverty gives you permission to hunger, to hope, to grow.

But false richness traps you in a life where **you can't even admit you're not okay.**

When Arup was younger, he too fell for the illusion.

He once leased a car he couldn't afford just to "look the part" at investor meetings. He dined at restaurants where he couldn't pronounce the wines, not because he enjoyed it, but because that's where "winners" were seen.

For years, he was rich in ambition but poor in **alignment.**

Until one day, at a café in Delhi, he saw a barefoot boy playing with a kite made from scrap plastic and string. The boy laughed—freely, fully, without care for the people watching.

In that moment, Arup asked himself:

"Why am I chasing a version of rich that makes me envy a child with nothing?"

He realised he had become a prisoner in a castle of perception.

The Real Danger: Silence

The illusion of being rich is dangerous not because it fools the world—but because it eventually **fools you.**

You stop asking for help because you're "not supposed to need it."

You stop being vulnerable because your "image" can't afford the crack.

You keep running because if you stop, the **truth might catch up.**

But what is the cost of a life where **you are not allowed to be real?**

Beyond the Illusion

True wealth is quiet. It doesn't need validation.

It sits in rooms where nothing flashy exists, but peace is **palpable.**

It's the kind of richness that lets you sleep well, not because your mattress is expensive, but because **your conscience is clear.**

True Poverty Is Misalignment

The greatest poverty is **disconnection from self.**

You could have seven figures and still cry yourself to sleep.

You could own three businesses and feel utterly unfulfilled.

You could travel the world and still be lost internally.

Because the soul does not respond to digits.

It responds to **truth.**

And any version of success that is out of alignment with your truth—**is failure in disguise.**

In his own journey, Arup found that true wealth wasn't about acquiring—it was about **remembering.**

Remembering his peace wasn't up for auction.

Remembering that he wasn't born to prove anything.

Remembering that **richness without presence is noise**.

And **poverty with purpose is sometimes the richer road**.

He left behind the chase for impression and returned to the craft of **essence**.

The illusion of being rich builds walls.

The experience of actual poverty builds perspective.

One isolates you in silence.

The other invites you to rise with truth.

Real power begins not when you can buy more—but when you no longer need to.

Because the ultimate luxury isn't a brand name.

It's **being able to live your truth without apology**.

The Unseen Currency: Redefining Richness through Freedom and Access

The Illusion of Having Everything—But Not Owning Yourself

Arup once met an old friend named Ishan at an international airport. Ishan had made it big. His LinkedIn glowed with achievements. His suitcase wheels glided over polished tiles like he owned the terminal.

But Arup noticed something in his tone: every word was rushed. Every breath, borrowed. Even his smile seemed outsourced.

Over coffee, Ishan confessed:

"I have more money than time to spend it. I can buy anything… except a day off. Isn't that strange?"

Strange. But not uncommon.

We've been conditioned to define richness as accumulation—of money, things, symbols. But what if the *truest* form of richness is **access**?

No access to things.

But access to **choice**.

To **stillness**.

To **moments**.

To **yourself**.

The Door That Opens Inward

Imagine two houses.

One is massive—a mansion with chandeliers, gates, and alarms. But every door is locked. You can see beauty through the glass, but you can't touch it. You're a guest in your own life.

The other is small, perhaps humble. But every door opens. To the kitchen. To the bedroom. To the garden. Most importantly—**to the self.**

Richness is not the mansion.

It's the **unlocked door.**

The ability to move freely.

To step into your life, not just watch it from behind bars of expectation or exhaustion.

When Arup Chose Stillness Over Status

A few years ago, Arup was offered a high-profile position at a multinational company. Lavish salary. Prestige. Power. Everything he had once thought he wanted.

But something in him hesitated.

He imagined the commute. The emails. The calendar. The loss of his morning walks. The silence he'd have to sacrifice. The writing he'd never finish. The moments with his ageing parents he'd miss.

He realised: **he'd be rich in currency, but bankrupt in access**—to his truth, his time, his art.

He turned the offer down.

Many called it foolish.

But Arup would later say:

"It was the first time I felt truly wealthy—not because of what I had, but because I could choose *not* to have what would cost me my soul."

Redefining Richness: The Quiet Freedoms

Real richness is the ability to:

- **Rest** without guilt.
- **Create** without pressure.
- **Say no** without fear.
- **Be present** without distraction.
- **Choose** without chains.

It's not just about what fills your bank account, but what fills your day, your breath, your being.

Access: The Forgotten Wealth

Access means:

- Having the time to attend your child's school play.
- Having the energy to sit in silence and hear your own thoughts.
- Having the autonomy to take a nap on a Tuesday, not because you're lazy, but because your body asked.

- Having the freedom to walk away from what's not aligned—without begging anyone for permission.

The Deeper Truth

Wealth that is only financial is still a form of servitude if it costs you freedom.

But richness that includes choice, presence, and peace—that's *sovereignty*.

This is what the world forgets to measure.

Not how many digits in your account.

But how many moments do you truly live?

Not what you can afford.

But what you're no longer forced to **endure***.*

A Question to Sit With

As you rise in the world…

Ask not only: *What am I gaining?*

But also: *What am I giving up to get there?*

Because real wealth is not in the flex.

It's in the **freedom to pause**.

To **breathe fully**.

To **live deliberately**.

The High Price of a Narrow Richness

When Rich Means Hollow

In a gleaming glass tower overlooking the city skyline, Arup sat across from a client named Riaan. The room smelled of leather and luxury. Everything about the office screamed success—yet the man behind the desk looked like a ghost wearing a Rolex.

Riaan had built empires. He had yachts, homes on three continents, and employees who called him "sir" more often than his children called him "dad."

His voice cracked over a sentence that lingered too long in Arup's ears:

"I won everything… except myself."

That was the moment Arup understood:

There is a kind of poverty that masquerades as richness.

The Golden Cage

Imagine a bird in a golden cage. It's fed exotic seeds, its feathers groomed, its perch encrusted with gems.

But it does not fly.

Every day, people pass by, admiring its beauty, its shimmer, its stillness. They say, "How lucky this bird is!"

But the bird does not sing anymore.

Why?

Because the cage, no matter how lavish, has stolen the sky.

This is what happens when we chase a narrow definition of wealth—one that glitters, but does not give us room to breathe.

Arup's Mirror Moment

There was a time when Arup, too, was caught in the rush. Bigger deals, bigger stage, faster growth. He was applauded everywhere—yet strangely alone in the applause. He missed birthdays. He skipped sunsets. He forgot the last time he sat in silence, not strategy.

One evening, after a talk that ended in a standing ovation, he returned to his hotel and looked in the mirror.

He didn't recognise the man staring back.

Tired eyes. An ache he couldn't name. A smile that felt… rented.

He sat on the bed, loosened his tie, and whispered aloud:

"What's the point of arriving at the top… if I've lost everything, I was meant to bring with me?"

It was the start of his awakening.

The Real Costs: What We Don't Put On the Balance Sheet

When we reduce richness to bank balances and lifestyle markers, we forget to account for what we silently spend along the way:

Emotional Cost:

Chronic stress. Burnout masked as ambition. The numbness that follows when joy becomes transactional. We hustle for validation and forget how to feel—how to *be*.

Spiritual Cost:

We trade soul for strategy. We silence our intuition to follow metrics. We forget what we *value* in the chase to become someone *valued*.

Relational Cost:

The missed calls. The drifting friendships. The partner who grows tired of being "scheduled in." Children who grow up learning that we're always busy "for them," but never really *with* them.

The Great Lie We're Sold

We are told that to be rich means to win.

But often, in that narrow race to win:

- We *lose* presence.
- We *lose* wonder.
- We *lose* the gentle parts of us that made life meaningful before we put a price tag on it.

True wealth was never meant to be heavy. It was meant to feel like freedom—not performance.

Redefining the Metrics

We must begin to ask better questions.

Not:

- *How much do I earn?*
- *What does my title say?*
- *What's next on the ladder?*

But:

- *Do I wake up at peace?*
- *Do I have the time to sit with my thoughts?*
- *Can I give to others without losing myself?*

Because if your version of being rich leaves you spiritually bankrupt, emotionally exhausted, and relationally isolated—then it is not richness. It's a mirage.

A Soft Reminder from Arup's Journal

In a quiet village, years later, Arup wrote in his journal:

"The richest moments of my life were the ones I couldn't post, couldn't invoice, couldn't brand. They were felt in full presence. With my father's hand in mine. With the monsoon winds hitting my face. With a poem whispered to myself before dawn.

That… was wealth."

Reflection

What have you traded in your chase for "richness"?

Is the price worth it?

And if not—what would it look like to reclaim the wealth that no one can deposit or withdraw, but only *live*?

CHAPTER III

What Is Wealth?

"Wealth is not about having more—it's about needing less and owning your time."

– Shree Shambav

Synopsis

What Is Wealth? Expands the reader's perspective beyond traditional definitions tied to money. It introduces wealth as a multidimensional state—measured not just in assets but in time, freedom, peace, and legacy. Emotional intelligence, spiritual depth, and intellectual curiosity are framed as core wealth-builders, often more impactful than bank balances. The idea of compounding is explored as a quiet superpower—not just in finance but in relationships, habits, and personal growth. This section empowers readers to focus on what truly endures: a life rich in meaning, not just money.

The Invisible Currency: Time, Freedom, and Peace

The Illusion of the Overflowing Cup

In the city of endless ambition, Arup once walked into a home where everything shimmered.

Marble floors. Chandeliers so grand they seemed to sigh under their own weight. A garage full of cars with names people whispered like a prayer.

The host, Dinesh, poured them a drink. He smiled often—but it was the kind of smile you see at a farewell, not a celebration.

"I built everything," he said, gesturing to his empire.

"But I have no time to sit inside what I built. No freedom to leave it. And peace? I don't even remember what that feels like."

That night, Arup walked home in silence.

Because it was there, in that fortress of gold, that he witnessed one of life's cruellest ironies:

You can **own everything** and **possess nothing** of true value.

The Garden with Locked Gates

Imagine two people.

One has the most exquisite garden. Rare orchids. A fountain that sings. A sky untouched by smoke.

But the garden is surrounded by locked gates, thick walls, and guards. He can only look at it through a security feed.

The other has a humble patch of earth. A few marigolds. A tree that gives shade. Birds that visit without invitation. She walks barefoot on its soil every morning.

Who is richer?

The first owns beauty.

The second **experiences** it.

And that is the point:

Real wealth is not in what we keep. It's in what we *feel*, *live*, and *breathe*.

Arup's Turning Point

There was a time when Arup worked twelve-hour days, seven days a week. He convinced himself it was temporary. "Just for a few more years," he'd say. "Then I'll slow down."

But the years stacked like bricks. So did the exhaustion.

One day, his niece Meera—no more than six—held his hand and asked softly:

"Why do you always come home tired, Arup-anna? (brother) Is that what big people do when they win?"

That question broke something open in him.

It was the gentlest rebellion.

He didn't sleep that night. Instead, he stared out the window and asked himself a haunting question:

"If the cost of my success is my life… then what exactly am I succeeding at?"

The Deeper Metrics of True Wealth

Let us redefine wealth, not by digits, but by **depth**:

Time

- Time to pause between thoughts.
- Time to be with your child without checking your phone.
- Time to *do nothing*—and not feel guilty.

Freedom

- Freedom to walk away from what drains you.
- Freedom to create, to say "no," to rest.
- Freedom to live aligned with who you are—not who you're expected to be.

Peace

- Peace that isn't conditional.
- Peace that lets you sleep, not escape.
- Peace that comes from knowing you're *enough*, even when the world claps elsewhere.

Income Is a Tool. Not the Truth.

Yes, money matters. It feeds, shelters, and enables.

But when we confuse income with identity, when we see possessions as personality, we begin to sacrifice the essential for the impressive.

We work to afford vacations we're too tired to enjoy.

We buy houses so big we grow distant inside them.

We accumulate—but never arrive.

The goal was never *just* to earn more.

The goal was to feel more *alive*.

A Scene from Arup's Rebirth

Years after that night with Meera, Arup had made changes. He worked less, created more. He no longer chased—he chose.

He began waking before dawn—not to check emails, but to greet the sunrise.

He'd brew tea, sit on the terrace, and write poetry. The silence wasn't empty anymore. It was full—of presence, with peace.

One morning, Meera sat beside him, legs swinging over the edge.

"You smile more now, Arup-anna."

He looked at her, eyes soft.

"I have more to smile about. I have *time* to smile."

What Wealth Really Means

Real wealth is not a loud life—it's a **liberated** one.

One where you can:

- Pause and listen to the rain.
- Say yes to dinner with old friends.
- Walk away from noise that doesn't nourish you.
- Build not for applause, but for legacy.

You are not truly wealthy if you cannot *feel* your days.

Because in the end, no one asks, "How much did you earn?"

They ask:

- "Did you love well?"
- "Did you live fully?"
- "Did you leave something behind that made the world softer?"

A Final Whisper from Arup's Heart

"I thought being rich meant more.

I learned that being rich meant enough.

Time to live it.

Freedom to choose it.

Peace to receive it."

The Hidden Pillars of True Prosperity

> "Not all treasures are kept in vaults. Some are grown in silence."

In a society that worships numbers—net worth, follower count, income brackets—there's a quieter economy. It doesn't show up on spreadsheets, but it builds the kind of wealth that *lasts*.

It is made of **emotional depth, spiritual grounding,** and **intellectual curiosity.**

These are not optional accessories to success.

They are its **foundation.**

Arup's Quiet Collapse

Arup had built an empire by 38. Multi-city businesses. A home his ancestors would've bowed before. On the surface, he was a success story.

But inside? He was fraying.

One evening, during a boardroom meeting, a simple disagreement triggered an outburst. He slammed the table. Walked out.

That night, he sat alone, hands trembling.

"Why am I always on edge? I have everything."

But that was the illusion.

He had *built*, yes.

But without the scaffolding of emotional regulation, without the compass of spiritual clarity, without the fuel of continuous intellectual engagement—his structure was hollow.

He had accumulated assets.

But he hadn't cultivated wealth.

Three Wells in a Desert

Imagine a man crossing a desert. He carries gold. Jewels. But no water.

He finds three wells:

- One brims with **emotional water**—the ability to soothe, to process, to relate.
- One glows with **spiritual light**—meaning, faith, the strength to endure.
- One overflows with **intellectual flow**—ideas, innovation, mental nourishment.

He can ignore them and keep chasing a city that may not exist.

Or he can drink deeply—and walk with strength, clarity, and imagination.

Material assets buy the journey.

Invisible wealth ensures you survive it.

Emotional Wealth: The Soil of Resilience

Emotional assets are often unglamorous.

They're the calm in conflict.

The pause before reacting.

The grace to forgive.

The self-trust to navigate uncertainty.

Arup began therapy. Started journaling. Learned to sit with discomfort instead of masking it with work or applause.

He realised that resilience isn't about brute strength. It's about being *soft* without breaking.

"My business didn't fail when I lost money.

It almost failed when I lost *myself*."

Spiritual Wealth: The Compass in Chaos

When Arup's father passed, nothing in his strategy books helped. He was lost—not financially, but existentially.

He met an old monk in a village near Kanchipuram who said:

"Your soul is thirsty, Arup. You've fed your ambition, but not your silence."

That sentence became a turning point.

He returned to ancient practices. Daily stillness. Gratitude. Service.

Not to *gain*, but to *remember*.

His decisions became clearer. His presence deeper.

He realised: *spirituality isn't about escape—it's about anchoring.*

Intellectual Wealth: The Engine of Expansion

Even after success, Arup remained a learner.

He studied philosophy, neuroscience, poetry. Not for a certificate—but to keep his mind sharp, supple, and hungry.

In meetings, he started asking better questions.

In life, he saw patterns—why some people repeated pain, why some breakthroughs were silent.

Intellectual wealth isn't just knowledge.

It's the **imagination** to create, adapt, and uplift others.

His team noticed. So did his children.

He was no longer the smartest in the room—he was the most curious.

And that made him the wisest.

True Prosperity Is Layered

Let's redefine prosperity as a **three-layered tree**:

- **Roots (Spiritual)** – Unseen, but everything depends on them. Purpose. Presence. Peace.
- **Soil (Emotional)** – The medium through which growth happens. Feelings, maturity, depth.
- **Leaves & Fruit (Intellectual)** – Ideas. Creativity. Solutions. Insight.

You can't skip the roots and expect the tree to last.

Arup's Legacy

Years later, Arup stood before a group of young dreamers.

He didn't show slides of revenue.

He told them stories:

- Of how his most valuable wealth was learning to **cry without shame**.
- Of how his greatest clarity came when he sat beneath a banyan tree and asked: *What really matters?*
- Of how every time he chose stillness over speed, or wisdom over ego—something magical aligned.

He ended with:

"If you build success without building yourself, you'll spend your whole life chasing what your soul can't hold. But if you build *within*, then no matter what changes outside—you rise."

True prosperity isn't what you flash in public.

It's what **holds you** in private.

When the world quiets, and the applause fades—

Your emotional wholeness, your spiritual peace, and your intellectual fire become the only wealth that matters.

"The Hidden Engine: Compounding and the Art of Becoming"

Most people understand compounding as a financial concept: invest a little, wait long enough, and watch it grow.

But what they miss is this:

Compounding is not a math trick.

It's a law of life.

And when truly understood, it doesn't just grow your money—

It grows your relationships, your habits, your wisdom, and even your legacy.

Arup and the Fruitless Mango Tree

When Arup was a child, his grandfather planted a mango sapling behind their home in Kanchipuram. Every summer, Arup would run to check if it had borne fruit. Year after year—nothing.

He grew impatient. "This tree is useless," he told his grandfather.

But the old man smiled and said,

"Some things grow down before they grow up."

He explained that the tree was developing roots. Quietly. Faithfully. Out of sight.

A few years later, the tree exploded with fruit. And every year after that, it offered more—without demand, without fail.

Decades later, Arup would remember this lesson not as a tale of gardening, but of **life, leadership, and wealth**.

Compounding in Money: The Slow Burn That Becomes a Blaze

When Arup entered the business world, he wanted fast wins. Quick profits. Big leaps.

He succeeded—but burned out.

Later, under the mentorship of an old investor named Dev, he was taught a different game.

Dev said,

"Compound interest doesn't just reward the clever. It rewards the **consistent**. It's not the size of the seed, Arup, but your patience with the season."

Arup began making modest but steady investments. The results didn't amaze anyone at first.

But over the years, the growth became exponential—not just in wealth, but in *confidence*.

Every disciplined choice he made added a brick to his future freedom.

Compounding in Relationships: Tiny Acts of Trust

When Arup was rebuilding bridges with his estranged brother, he remembered something a monk once said:

"Love does not arrive fully grown. It is watered in silence."

He began with a call. Then a letter. Then showing up.

Each effort felt small. But each built upon the last.

Trust, like money, compounds—**especially when you don't demand instant return.**

Years later, their bond became stronger than it ever was.

Not because of a grand apology. But because of the **steady rhythm of commitment**.

Compounding in Habits: Becoming Who You Were Meant to Be

We often overestimate the power of one massive action. —and underestimate the power of tiny, repeated steps.

Arup began waking up 30 minutes earlier each day to journal, meditate, or read.

Just 30 minutes.

That's it.

But over the years?

- He healed old wounds through journaling.
- He gained clarity through stillness.
- He absorbed the wisdom of over 100 books.

None of it was dramatic on a single day.

But together?

It made him unshakable.

"Success," he wrote in his notebook,

"isn't built in hours. It's built in heartbeats—accumulated with care."

Compounding in Wisdom: The Snowball of Insight

At 40, Arup met a retired physicist named Raghavan who said:

"Wisdom compounds not with time, but with reflection."

Every mistake Arup had made—every triumph, every failure—became fertiliser for deeper understanding.

As he revisited old memories with new eyes, he began to see patterns.

- Why did some people kept rising.
- Why he had fallen at times despite external success.
- Why the most powerful people were often the most still.

What once seemed random began to make sense.

He wasn't just ageing.

He was **compounding**—mentally, spiritually, emotionally.

The Bamboo Forest

In China, bamboo trees are planted and watered daily. For years, nothing happens.

Then suddenly—**in the fifth year**—they grow **90 feet in just six weeks**.

Did the bamboo grow in six weeks?

No.

It grew in five years.

Underground. Unseen. Silent.

This is the truth of compounding.

You're either growing roots—or giving up before the miracle.

The Real Currency of Compounding

Anyone can have a windfall.

But only those who honour the slow, sacred rhythm of growth—who return to their craft, their calling, their relationships, their practices *again and again*—experience the **deep harvest**.

In Arup's final speech to a group of aspiring changemakers, he said:

"Every small action you repeat with love becomes your signature.
Every word you say with care becomes your character.

Every moment you honour becomes your legacy.

Compounding is the universe rewarding you for **consistency with your soul**."

The Silent Force Behind Greatness

So why is compounding central to long-term wealth?

Because time favours the patient.

The universe trusts the faithful.

And life ultimately belongs not to those who sprint once—

But to those who **walk with purpose**, every day, without applause, into the greatness that is already unfolding.

"From Applause to Alignment: Arup's Journey to Inner Prosperity"

In the flickering glow of dusk, Arup stood before a crowd of thousands. He had been awarded yet another title, this time *Visionary of the Year*. Applause rang loud. Cameras flashed. But as he stood there—smiling on the outside—he felt an emptiness inside that couldn't be named.

That night, in his quiet suite, he stared at the glass of wine he hadn't touched and whispered to himself:

"Why doesn't this feel like it used to?"

The Illusion of Applause

For years, Arup had chased excellence—and with it, validation.
Every achievement, every article written about him, every social media post that went viral, fed a hunger. But like a meal made of fog, it never truly nourished.

He thought success was the applause.

But in chasing it, he became a performer in his own life.

Like a bird trained to sing for coins, he had mistaken the cage of praise for the sky of freedom.

The Mirror Moment: Meeting Bhairavi

On a spontaneous trip to the Himalayas, Arup met Bhairavi, a former investment banker turned monk. She offered him tea brewed with herbs she had grown herself and asked, without any ceremony:

"Who are you when no one is watching?"

He laughed nervously, listing his achievements.

She interrupted gently:

"I didn't ask for your résumé. I asked about your **root**."

He didn't have an answer. Not an honest one.

The Shift: From Performance to Presence

That night, under a sky full of stars that didn't care about his titles, Arup cried.

He cried not out of failure, but realisation:

He had built a palace for the world, but a hut for his soul.

The applause had become his oxygen. But now he could barely breathe in silence.

So, he began again. Not with goals. But with grounding.

Step by Step: Cultivating Inner Prosperity

Bhairavi taught him three practices—not strategies, but **ways of being**:

1. **Silence Over Signal**

    Every morning, Arup sat without a phone, without a schedule. Just breath.

    At first, it was agonising. He felt useless. But slowly, he began hearing the voice he had long ignored—his own.

2. **Service Without Stage**

    Bhairavi assigned him small, invisible acts of service—cleaning, cooking for others, tending to the garden. No one praised him. No one noticed.

    And in that anonymity, he discovered something new: peace.

3. Joy Without Justification

He began painting again. He danced under the moonlight. He wrote poetry that no one would read.

He lived—not to prove—but to express.

The Candle and the Lighthouse

Validation is like a candle. It glows bright, but melts quickly. It needs protection. And when the wind of criticism blows, it flickers and dies.

But inner prosperity is a **lighthouse**.

It stands still, even in storms. It does not beg for attention. It **guides**, not glitters.

Arup had spent years lighting candles in every room, but never built his lighthouse.

Now, brick by brick—through silence, service, stillness—he was constructing it.

The Return: Same World, Different Centre

Arup eventually returned to the world of influence—but this time, **he wasn't performing**.

He *didn't post every success.*

He *said no to stages that drained him.*

He *mentored not to be seen, but to truly serve.*

And when someone asked, "What drives you now?"

He smiled and said,

"Before, I was chasing mirrors. Now, I'm rooted in the soil. I grow because it's my nature—not for the applause."

Inner Prosperity: The Only Wealth That Cannot Be Taken

- Titles fade.
- Accolades get replaced.
- Even the loudest applause eventually stops.

But the richness of knowing who you are, the quiet joy of alignment, the calm of walking your truth?

That sustains. That heals. That lasts.

The Invitation

To anyone chasing external validation—Arup would say this:

"You're not here to impress the world.

*You're here to **remember your own light**.*

*The world needs more people who are **rooted**, not just visible.*

Create from joy. Serve from love. Rest in truth.

And watch as the world begins to reflect back the wholeness you've cultivated within."

Because the applause may come.

Or it may not.

*But when you're **aligned**—You no longer need it to know you've already arrived.*

CHAPTER IV

Rich vs. Wealthy vs. Powerful

A man with money and no purpose is still poor. A leader with power and no peace is still lost."

— *Shree Shambav*

Synopsis

Rich vs. Wealthy vs. Powerful presents a nuanced exploration of three often-interchanged ideas, revealing why they must not be confused. It shows how each—riches, wealth, and power—plays a distinct role in the architecture of a fulfilling life. Through relatable case studies and real-world contrasts, readers discover what happens when one pillar is strong while the others are ignored. Some have riches but no freedom, some wield influence but lack peace, and others are wealthy in spirit yet unseen by society. This section offers a compass to navigate toward a more balanced and holistic version of success, one that lasts beyond trends, applause, or market shifts.

The Three Gates: Richness, Wealth, and Power

Arup had made his first million by thirty-two.

It came with the usual trappings: a penthouse overlooking the skyline, a luxury car he rarely drove, an investment portfolio managed by men in suits who spoke in acronyms. People called him "rich," and for a while, he wore that title like a crown.

But deep down, something didn't sit right.

Gate One: The Realm of the Rich

Being **rich** was about accumulation.

Arup noticed that this form of success felt fragile. His richness was **loud**, constantly needing to be fed—new watches, new vacations, new validations. He began to realise that being rich was like owning a **fountain with no reservoir**. Water flows impressively, but it needs a continuous pump. The moment income slowed, so did his sense of identity.

He met others at this gate: men and women whose money screamed, but whose hearts whispered. Some feared losing what they had. Others were too exhausted to enjoy it. It was a beautiful cage with velvet bars.

Then he met Rafiq.

Gate Two: The Domain of the Wealthy

Rafiq owned fewer things but lived with **immense spaciousness**—time to think, presence to play with his children, freedom to say no without guilt.

He told Arup:

"Being **wealthy** is not about what you have. It's about what you can afford to walk away from."

Wealth was not loud. It was **quiet and unshakable**. It lived in health, peace of mind, and relationships that weren't based on transactions. It was the kind of richness that allowed a person to take a day off **without feeling poor**.

Arup saw the difference. Richness was **visible**. Wealth was **felt**. Richness needed to be updated. Wealth aged gracefully.

He realised wealth was when your **life** earned as much as your money did.

But something was still missing.

Gate Three: The Sphere of Power

It was only after a soul-altering experience in Kumbhariyur, where he sat for days in silence with a spiritual teacher, that Arup understood **power**.

Power, he discovered, had nothing to do with domination or command.

"Real power," the Guru (Master) said, "is your ability to **remain rooted in truth**—to act without needing permission, to lead without needing followers, to move mountains by moving **yourself** first."

This was **inner authority**.

Power meant not reacting, but choosing.

Not influencing others through fear, but through presence.

Not needing a spotlight, because your **light couldn't be dimmed**.

It was here that Arup saw the full picture.

Arup once threw a grand party in a glass house on a hill. Rich people came, music played, and champagne flowed.

Ten years later, he hosted a quiet retreat by a river. Only a handful came—friends, thinkers, seekers. They meditated at dawn, cooked together, and shared life's truths by the fire.

He later wrote in his journal:

"The house on the hill showed people who I was trying to be. The retreat by the river revealed who I truly am."

Why Confusing Them Leads to Imbalance

- When we **chase richness**, we mistake noise for meaning. Life becomes performative. Exhaustion becomes inevitable.
- When we **settle only for wealth**, we may secure comfort but miss impact.
- And when we **grasp at power** without grounding, it turns into manipulation or burnout.

The Distinctions

Aspect	Rich	Wealthy	Powerful
Source	Money (External)	Time + Choice + Peace (Internal/External)	Awareness + Alignment (Internal)
Sound	Loud	Quiet	Resonant
Dependency	Needs performance	Needs structure	Needs truth
Fear	Losing status	Losing stability	Losing self-control

Freedom	Limited	Expansive	Sovereign
Impact	Impresses	Sustains	Transforms

But when these three align—**richness supported by wealth, governed by true power**—we become **whole**.

We don't just live successfully.

We live **meaningfully**.

There's a parable told by an elder in the village of Kumbhariyur:

"A man came to the temple and said, 'I want to be rich.' The sage replied, 'Then earn.'

He returned and said, 'I want to be wealthy.'

The sage smiled, 'Then learn to let go.'

He finally asked, 'I want to be powerful.'

The sage looked into his eyes and whispered,

'Then remember who you are when there's no one left to impress.'"

The Unravelling: When Success Stands on One Leg

Imagine success as a sacred fire built with three kinds of wood: **riches, power,** and **wealth**—not just in money, but in meaning, impact, and peace.

When one of these is missing, the fire flickers. When two are gone, it smokes and suffocates. And when all you have is one… it might look bright for a moment, but it doesn't last the night.

Let's step into three real-world stories. Different people. Same lesson: Success that's lopsided will, eventually, collapse under its own weight.

1. The Man with Everything—Except Meaning

Name: X

Had: Riches

Lacked: Influence, Legacy, Inner Fulfilment

X was a Wall Street titan. Billionaire by 42. His face appeared on the covers of Forbes and Fortune. His kids went to Ivy League schools, his yacht docked in Monaco, and his watches cost more than most people's homes.

And yet, when he turned 50, he couldn't sleep. Not insomnia—emptiness.

His daughter once said on a podcast, *"He built an empire but forgot to build himself into it."*

He was rich, but not remembered—respected, but not loved. When he retired, no one called. When he gave talks, people nodded politely but never quoted him. He had **no legacy**, because legacy is not minted in gold, but in hearts moved, minds awakened, and lives touched.

He bought the world but couldn't buy it worth.

2. The Leader with Power—But No Peace

Name: Y

Had: Power

Lacked: Emotional Wealth, Connection

Y was a political force. Her policies transformed entire districts. Her face was known across newsrooms, her decisions echoed in boardrooms. She rose from nothing—grit, brilliance, vision.

But at home? Silence. Her husband, estranged. Her children, distant. Her soul, parched.

She once confessed during a quiet off-the-record interview:

"I can move nations. But I can't move my own heart anymore. I forgot how to be gentle with myself."

She had **power without peace**, and it corroded her from within. Her speeches became more polished, but her eyes dimmed. People feared her more than they followed her. She was influential, yes. But no longer inspiring.

She had a throne, but not a sanctuary.

3. The Man with Wisdom—But No Foundation

Name: Z

Had: Wealth of wisdom and spiritual depth

Lacked: Financial Security and Strategic Power

Z was a poet, a spiritual teacher. His words healed trauma, his presence disarmed pain. People came to his satsangs in droves. But behind the curtains, he struggled to pay rent.

He saw money as impure, forgetting that energy, in any form, is neutral—it flows based on alignment and stewardship.

A disciple once asked him why he didn't monetise his teachings.
He whispered, *"I worry it would corrupt me."*

But the truth? **The lack of money limited the spread of his light.**

He had a wealth of soul, but no structure to carry it beyond his lifetime. No team. No plan. No reach. His words lived in air, not in archives. When he died, much of his legacy died with him.

He built truth, but not a channel for it.

The Bridge Is Integration

Now, let's contrast these with someone who integrated all three: **A conscious entrepreneur and teacher.**

He wasn't the richest man in the room, but he **owned his time**.

He wasn't the loudest leader, but his words shaped decisions. He wasn't chasing status, but **he walked in stillness**, and that stillness moved people more than strategy.

He built:

- **Financial stability**—but only from things that aligned with his soul.
- **Influence**—but not through manipulation; through presence.
- **Peace**—that didn't make him passive, but profoundly powerful.

He used money as a servant, not a master. Power as a light, not a weapon. Wealth as a platform, not a pedestal.

The Core Insight

Success **unravels** when one thread carries the burden of the entire fabric.

- Riches without wisdom become vanity.
- Power without peace becomes tyranny.
- Spiritual wealth without strategy becomes forgotten poetry.

You don't need all three **at once**, but you do need to **intentionally cultivate the triad**—in your own rhythm, with your own compass.

Because *true success* isn't how far you go—it's how deeply you're rooted when you get there.

The Root Beneath the Tower: Choosing the Right Foundation

We often build our lives like we build monuments—upward, not inward.

We chase **riches** first, believing they will solve our restlessness.
We chase **power**, thinking it will protect our position.
We chase the symbols, the stage, the applause.

But rarely do we pause and ask:

What am I standing on?

Because if the foundation is fragile, no matter how high we climb, it will crumble. And the question isn't whether it will—it's when.

The Three Pillars: Power, Riches, Wealth

To understand which lays the strongest foundation for lasting fulfilment, we must first understand how they differ at their core.

- **Riches** are about **what you have**.

Money, assets, luxuries.

They are *external* and *quantifiable*.

- **Power** is about **what you can do**.

Influence, access, decision-making.

It is *positional* and often *conditional*.

- **Wealth**—true wealth—is about **who you are and how you live**.

It's time-freedom, emotional clarity, spiritual depth, relationships, health, legacy.

It is *internal, invisible,* and often *unnoticed until it's gone.*

Now ask: Which of these do you want to **stand on** for the next 40 years?

The Story of Arup: The Sequence That Saved Him

Arup was once a young professional chasing riches.

He was in his twenties when he landed a dream tech job. Six-figure salary. Fast promotions. A corner office by 30. His social media looked like a highlight reel—vacations, watches, a designer lifestyle. But beneath it? Quiet anxiety. Shallow friendships. A gnawing sense that none of this *meant* anything.

At 32, Arup had a panic attack before a board meeting. His heart pounded not from stress, but from **emptiness**.

That night, he wrote in his journal: *"If this is success, why do I feel like I'm dying inside?"*

He quit the next month. Everyone thought he was crazy.

But he wasn't quitting success. He was **rebuilding it—on a new foundation**.

He began with *internal wealth*:

- Meditation.
- Community.
- Creative expression.
- Deep rest.
- Long conversations with wise elders.
- Learning to cook, to forgive, to sit in silence.

From this wealth of being, **clarity arose**.

He started a mission-driven venture, not just a business. He learned to use power not as dominance but as stewardship. Money returned—but this time it felt light, not heavy.

Arup didn't abandon riches or power. He just chose to sequence them after wealth.

The Danger of Getting the Sequence Wrong

Let's flip the story.

Someone begins with riches. They buy freedom, but they don't know what to do with it. They accumulate, but remain insecure. The void inside grows. Eventually, the lifestyle becomes a prison—golden, but still a cage.

Or someone begins with power. They lead with force, dominate through fear, rise quickly. But they trust no one. Relationships are transactions. The empire they build becomes a glass tower: shiny on the outside, but cracks with the first storm.

*Without **wealth of self**, power becomes tyranny.*

*Without a **wealth of spirit**, riches become an addiction.*

The Inner Wealth First Principle

True wealth isn't what you carry in your wallet. It's what you carry in your walk.

It's:

- Waking up without dread.
- Creating without fear.
- Loving without agenda.
- Giving without depletion.

- Resting without guilt.

And from that ground, you can build riches.

You can wield power.

Because now they are tools—not your identity.

The Lamp, the Oil, and the Flame

Imagine a traditional oil lamp.

- The **flame** is your power—it is seen, it illuminates.
- The **lamp's structure** is your riches—it holds the form.
- But without **oil**—your inner wealth—the flame dies, no matter how beautiful the lamp.

Too many today are flame-chasers. Few are oil-gatherers. But only one sustains.

What Do You Want to Endure?

Ask yourself not just what kind of life you want to **build**, but what kind of life you want to **wake up to**.

The most sustainable success is **wealth-first**:

- Then comes authentic power—rooted, not performed.
- Then come aligned riches—earned without self-erosion.

Because a life built on the wealth of the soul can bear the weight of any storm.

And that is not just a foundation—it's a fortress.

The Fragile House of One Pillar

Imagine a grand structure—a palace, perhaps—built on just one column. It might stand for a while, might even dazzle those passing by. But it lives on borrowed time.

Because identity that leans too far in one direction loses its centre.

Arup and the Weight of Riches

Arup's story, once again, reveals a deeper truth.

In his late twenties, Arup had accumulated wealth that most people only dreamt of. Stock options. Multiple properties. Passive income. A calendar full of investor meetings and startup pitches.

From the outside, he was "that guy." The golden boy. The young millionaire.

But what no one saw was this:

- He hadn't spoken to his father in two years.
- He couldn't remember the last time he cried—or laughed without checking his phone.
- His mornings began with screens, not silence.
- His friendships felt more like networking than nourishment.

Arup had built his identity on **riches**. And slowly, his soul began to suffocate beneath the weight of performance.

Then came the night he was honoured at a business conference. Standing under the spotlight, holding a glass trophy, he looked at the crowd, at the cameras flashing... and felt nothing.

No pride. No peace. Just a hollow ache that whispered, *"You've built an empire of applause, but no home for your heart."*

The Cost of an Unbalanced Identity

When identity is built only on **riches**, you live in constant fear of loss. Your worth is tied to your net worth. Every dip in the market feels like a personal collapse.

When identity is built only on **power**, you live in control and isolation. People obey, but few connect. Relationships become transactional, not transformational. Vulnerability becomes a threat.

When identity is built only on **wealth**—without engaging the world—you risk spiritual bypassing. You meditate but avoid action. You speak of love but shy from leadership. You feel good but don't grow impact.

True identity is not built on a single pillar. It is the sacred integration of **being**, **doing**, and **becoming**.

The Three-Legged Stool

Picture a stool with three legs.

- One leg is **riches**—resources, access, opportunity.
- One leg is **power**—influence, voice, reach.
- One leg is **inner wealth**—wisdom, love, purpose.

Remove one, and the stool wobbles. Sit long enough, and it will tip.

Now imagine sitting on that stool through the storms of life—loss, change, aging, heartbreak. Without all three, you'll fall. But with them, you remain steady.

Real-World Examples of Collapse

1. **The Celebrity Who Lost Himself**

A global icon once said in an interview, "I don't know who I am when the cameras turn off." His identity, built on fame and riches, became a mask too heavy to wear—and too dangerous to remove.

2. **The Executive Who Burned Out**

A powerful CEO controlled boardrooms but had no control over her anxiety. Her power isolated her. The people feared her—but no one truly *saw* her. When her health failed, so did her identity.

3. **The Spiritual Seeker Who Withdrew from Life**

A man who pursued only spiritual wealth retreated from the world. He was peaceful but poor, wise but disconnected, enlightened but irrelevant. He struggled with purpose beyond personal calm.

A Balanced Identity: The Truest Wealth

A fulfilled life invites all three elements into the room:

- **Riches** to fund dreams and serve others.
- **Power** to uplift, speak, and lead with courage.
- **Inner wealth** to navigate life with grace, humility, and joy.

When identity arises from **all three**, the soul finds peace.

The heart stays open.

The mind stays sharp.

And the life lived becomes a **legacy**, not just a lifestyle.

Final Reflection

Ask yourself: *If everything I owned was taken from me, who would I still be?*

If the world went quiet, and there were no metrics left—no likes, no salaries, no stages—*what part of me would still stand tall?*

That is where your real identity lives. That is where balance breathes. That is where lasting fulfilment is born—not in any single pillar, but in the harmony between them.

PART TWO

MINDSET - Shaping the Inner World

"Consumers chase trends. Creators shape worlds. Your rise begins the moment you choose to create."

- Shree Shambav

CHAPTER V

The Mind Behind the Rise

"Abundance isn't about what you own—it's about what you no longer fear."

— Shree Shambav

Synopsis

The Mind Behind the Rise explores the silent engine that powers everything—mindset. It draws a bold line between those who consume life and those who create it. Through the lens of creator vs. consumer, the content dives into how thinking patterns shape outcomes far more than circumstances do. It dissects scarcity thinking—how it hides behind overwork, envy, or control—and provides tools to shift toward abundant living. The importance of identity is spotlighted, revealing how people rise or fall based on the internal stories they believe. More than motivation, this section is a recalibration—a call to rewire the mind to rise with clarity, confidence, and conviction.

The Two Roads

In a small, sun-kissed town nestled between the hills and a river, lived Arup. In his early years, Arup, like many, lived in **consumer consciousness**. He absorbed. He followed. He waited.

- He scrolled through other people's lives.

- He read countless books but rarely applied their wisdom.

- He watched success from a distance, convinced it belonged to others who "had something he didn't."

He was brilliant, thoughtful, and full of ideas. But he was waiting for the *right time*, the *right approval*, the *perfect version of himself* to begin.

Until one evening, under the rustling neem tree where his grandfather used to sit, he found an old journal.

Inside was a single sentence:

"The river does not ask for permission to flow—it simply moves and creates paths."

It struck him like thunder in a quiet room.

That night, Arup sat in stillness and realised the harsh truth: He had become a collector of possibilities, not a creator of realities.

The Mindset of the Consumer

The **consumer** mindset is reactive, passive, and externally anchored. It survives by feeding on the creations of others.

- It waits for motivation instead of generating it.

- It shops for wisdom but rarely metabolises it into action.

- It seeks entertainment over engagement, validation over value, and trends over truth.

It says, "Let me see what others are doing before I move."

This mindset breeds dependence. It teaches the soul to look outward for worth, for permission, for direction. Over time, the consumer becomes a shadow—living life **secondhand**.

And here's the trap: In the age of content and convenience, consumerism isn't just about buying things. It's about outsourcing your own becoming.

The Mindset of the Creator

The **creator** mindset, in contrast, is alive, generative, and inwardly resourced.

- It looks within and asks, *"What can I bring to life from this experience?"*

- It values originality over imitation, initiation over perfection.

- It understands that power is not seized—but seeded, nurtured, and grown.

Creation doesn't always mean making art or building companies. Sometimes it's subtler:

- Choosing to **respond** instead of react.

- Turning pain into **poetry**, struggle into **story**, failure into **fuel**.

- Building not just a brand, but **a body of work** that is in conversation with the soul.

Creation is a posture, not a product. A way of relating to life, not just performing in it.

A consumer may gain success, but it will be borrowed. Fragile. Dependent on external engines.

A creator, on the other hand, builds success that reflects their soul. It endures because it flows from being, not from performing.

Creator vs. Consumer: The Levers of Power and Wealth

Trait	Consumer Mindset	Creator Mindset
Power	Seeks it in others	Generates it from alignment
Wealth	Spends and imitates	Builds and innovates
Influence	Chases trends	Sets the tone
Identity	Curated through others	Forged in truth
Fulfilment	Fleeting and dependent	Deep and self-generated

The Mirror Moment

There came a time when Arup stopped consuming content before bed. He began creating space—silence, journaling, sketching ideas. He wrote without knowing where it would go. He started conversations without scripting them. He stopped waiting to be ready.

Slowly, he became *a man in motion.*

People noticed—not because he marketed himself, but because something inside him was **lit**.

And one day, when asked how he became so "influential," he smiled and replied,

"I stopped asking the world what I was allowed to be, and started showing it what I already am."

The Garden vs. The Store

A **consumer** walks into the store of life and browses what's on offer. Chooses from what others have made. Pays a price. Leaves hungry for more.

A **creator** walks into a patch of land—perhaps empty, perhaps overgrown—and begins to **cultivate**.

- They plant seeds (ideas).
- They tend to the soil (inner beliefs).
- They water with action, sunlight with presence, and protect from weeds (distractions).

Over time, they don't just eat. They **feed others**. They don't just consume. They **nourish**.

The Path to Inner Sovereignty

In the end, the distinction is not just about how we make money or build power—it's about **who we become**.

The consumer is shaped by the world.

The creator *shapes* the world.

And when you shift from passive consumption to active creation, you reclaim not just your time—but your **destiny**.

Because true power is not earned by echoing others. It is built by becoming so rooted in your essence that the world cannot help but respond.

The Silent Saboteur: Scarcity in the Shadow of Success

Arup stood at the edge of the stage. The applause behind him had faded. The spotlight dimmed. Another award. Another headline. Another moment that felt... incomplete.

He wasn't ungrateful. He had come a long way—from the quiet boy who once doubted his voice to the man who now moved crowds. But in the stillness of hotel rooms, long after the curtain had closed, he often wrestled with a strange hunger. Not for more money. Not for more fame.

But for *enoughness*.

For peace.

And it was here, in this space of internal questioning, that Arup began to realise something startling:

Scarcity doesn't only live in the poor. Sometimes, it is most cunningly alive in the successful.

The Hidden Face of Scarcity Thinking

Scarcity is not just the fear of not having enough—it is the fear of *not being enough*.

High achievers often hide it behind ambition, productivity, or perfection. But look deeper, and you'll see it in the micro-moments:

- Saying yes when their soul screams no—because they fear losing relevance.
- Overpreparing for meetings—because they fear being seen as inadequate.
- Competing in rooms they've already outgrown—because they fear invisibility.
- Comparing silently—while publicly cheering others on.

This isn't drive. This is *disguised deprivation*.

Ambition vs. Scarcity: A Dangerous Confusion

Ambition rooted in **abundance** says:

"There is room for all of us. My rise does not threaten yours."

"I create because I'm full, not because I'm empty."

"I expand because life is meant to be expressed."

But ambition rooted in **scarcity** whispers:

"If I stop, I'll fall behind."

"If they win, I lose."

"If I don't do more, I'll become irrelevant."

Scarcity shrinks the soul while the outer world may be expanding. And eventually, that internal collapse shows up as burnout, anxiety, bitterness, or isolation.

Arup's Mirror Moment

It happened one evening, in the mountains of Himachal, where Arup had escaped for silence. He met a monk, who after listening quietly to Arup's restlessness, handed him a small copper bowl.

"Fill this with the river water," he said.

Arup brought it back, full.

Then the monk asked, "Now, carry it across the rocks without spilling. But with one change—walk while smiling and humming."

Arup tried, but he kept spilling. His face grew tense.

"You see," the monk said gently, "you were more focused on not losing water than on enjoying the walk. That is scarcity—living to *protect* what you have instead of *expanding* who you are."

The Tree vs. The Tank

Scarcity operates like a **water tank**—measuring drops, fearing leaks, always monitoring the level.

Abundance flows like a **tree**—drawing from deeper roots, growing, giving shade and fruit, not afraid of seasons. A tree doesn't say, "I must hoard my leaves for fear of winter." It *trusts the cycle.*

Likewise, true achievers in abundance:

- Trust their inner source more than external supply.
- Give without calculating loss.
- Celebrate others without diminishing themselves.
- Rest without guilt.

How to Shift from Scarcity to Abundance

1. **Awareness of Micro-Scarcity**

    - Notice where urgency, control, jealousy, or over-commitment creep in.
    - Ask: *"Is this action flowing from fear or fullness?"*

2. **Replace Comparison with Contribution**

    - Move from "How do I measure up?" to "How do I show up?"

3. **Root Identity in Essence, Not Output**

- Your worth is not your work. Your being is not your brand.

4. **Practice Spaciousness**
    - Say no.
    - Breathe before you react.
    - Take breaks without productivity guilt.

5. **Celebrate Enough**
    - Abundance often hides in simple, quiet, unmarketed moments: a hug, a shared meal, a fulfilled promise.

Legacy Beyond Lack

Arup later wrote in his journal:

"The world called me rich when I accumulated.

The soul called me abundant when I finally released.

In stillness, I remembered: I was never lacking—only disconnected."

True wealth is not the absence of scarcity but the *presence of knowing you're whole.*

Final Reflection

"Abundance is not something you chase. It's something you remember."

When achievers begin to rewire this truth—not just intellectually, but emotionally—they unlock a deeper form of success:

- One that heals instead of hustles.
- One that attracts rather than chases.
- One that leaves a legacy of freedom, not fear.

The Silent Sculptor: How Identity Carves the Arc of Destiny

Arup sat alone at the old tea shop near the riverbank in his childhood village. The place was quiet, save for the gentle rustle of peepul leaves and the occasional laughter of children playing nearby.

He had returned not for nostalgia, but for clarity.

He had built businesses, spoken on global stages, and mentored hundreds—but something invisible had begun tugging at his soul. Despite the achievements, a pattern kept repeating. He would rise... and then plateau. Open doors... and yet feel undeserving. Make money... and yet feel anxious.

Sipping the strong masala chai, Arup's mind wandered back to his grandfather's words:

"You are not just what you do. You are what you *believe* you are."

It was then that Arup understood:

Identity isn't just personal—it's foundational. It shapes every choice, every risk, every relationship, every transaction, and ultimately, every outcome.

The Invisible Code: Identity as Operating System

Think of identity as the **operating system** of the human experience. Everything else—goals, behaviours, habits—are just applications running on it. If the OS is coded with fear, lack, or shame, no matter how powerful the apps, the system will crash eventually.

Childhood scripts, cultural narratives, family dynamics, and formative failures all begin to write this silent code:

- "Money is hard to keep."
- "I have to prove my worth."
- "Success means sacrifice."
- "People like us don't become wealthy."
- "If I shine, I'll be alone."

These aren't just thoughts. They're **embedded identity statements**.

They become internal ceilings. You don't rise to your ambition—you rise to your **identity ceiling**.

Arup and the Two Mirrors

Arup once told a story during a retreat:

"There were two mirrors in a palace—one enchanted, the other real.

The real mirror reflected your face.
The enchanted one reflected your beliefs.

A poor man walked in.
The real mirror showed him as he was—dignified, strong.
But the enchanted mirror showed him hunched, timid, lesser.

He left the palace defeated.

The mirror didn't lie.
It revealed what he believed to be true.

And that, friends, is the tragedy of many lives. They live not who they are, but who they think they are."

How Early Identity Shapes Financial and Life Outcomes

1. **Risk Tolerance and Opportunity Recognition**

    If you subconsciously believe you don't deserve wealth, you will sabotage opportunities or not even *see* them.

2. **Financial Habits and Boundaries**

    Over-giving, under-earning, compulsive saving, or reckless spending often come from identity wounds around worth.

3. **Relationships and Negotiations**

    If you feel small, you settle. If you feel unseen, you overcompensate. Either way, your financial life bleeds.

4. **Creative Potential**

Your identity will tell you what's "appropriate" for someone like you. If you carry a "worker" identity, you may never allow yourself to become a visionary.

Reprogramming Identity: Rewriting the Internal Script

To shift identity is not to fake confidence—it is to **reclaim authorship** over your own narrative.

Here's how Arup began to rewire:

1. **Awareness of the Origin Stories**

    He journaled: *Where did I first feel I wasn't enough?*

    Whose voice told me I had to earn love or success?

2. **Emotional Reconciliation**

    He didn't just analyse. He grieved. He honoured the little boy who had survived with those beliefs. And he gently released him from duty.

3. **Identity Anchors**

    Instead of affirmations alone, Arup lived into new identity anchors:

    - "I am a generous steward of wealth."
    - "My voice opens doors—for myself and others."
    - "It is safe to expand."

4. **Embodied Action**

Every time he made a bold choice, said no with dignity, or invested in himself, he was not just changing his finances—he was reinforcing his identity.

The River and the Container

Money, love, and opportunity are like a river. But your identity is the container you carry to collect it.

If your inner vessel is cracked with doubt or small from shame, you'll walk away from the river saying, "See, there wasn't enough."

But the river was never the issue. Your container was.

Reflection

"We do not manifest what we want.

We manifest who we believe we are."

When people rewire their identity from survival to sovereignty, from lack to love, from shame to sacredness—their behaviour naturally shifts. And with it, their financial and life trajectories elevate.

Journaling Prompt for the Reader

"What identity did I inherit—and what identity will I now choose?"

Mindset: The Invisible Architecture of Destiny

In the town of Kanchipuram, Arup sat under the ancient neem tree, the same one his grandfather had once used as a resting spot during long walks. The soil beneath the tree was cracked, dry, and tired from the summer heat. Yet, the tree stood tall—branches outstretched, green and unwavering.

A young boy from the village, Aarav, asked, "How does it survive without rain, Anna(brother)?"

Arup smiled gently and answered,

"Because its roots are deep enough to drink from places your eyes cannot see."

And then, almost whispering, he added,

"Just like a true mindset."

Why Strategy Alone Doesn't Save Us

We live in an age obsessed with *strategies*.

- Hacks to scale.
- Frameworks to win.
- Scripts to close deals.
- Habits to become high-performing.

But here's the dangerous illusion:

Strategy without soul is scaffolding without structure.

Execution without elevation is just repetition in disguise.

You can *learn* a new behaviour, but if your internal identity, belief system, and emotional baseline haven't evolved, you will *always revert* to what you *feel safe* being—even if it sabotages your progress.

The Three Climbers

There were three climbers who set out to conquer a treacherous mountain. They all had the same gear, the same map, the same food, and the same weather conditions.

- The first one quit halfway—overwhelmed by the voices in his head saying, "You're not strong enough."
- The second one reached the top but fell while descending because his fear of losing what he gained took over.
- The third one, who had faced many internal mountains before this one, moved with calm rhythm, not just upward, but inward. He finished and returned, not just victorious, but transformed.

They all had a strategy. Only one had depth.

Mindset Is Not Motivation. It's the Operating Blueprint.

Motivation gets you going.

Mindset *decides* where you're going—and why.

Here's what most don't realise:

- You can be productive and still be rooted in fear.
- You can be busy and still feel like an impostor.

- You can hit goals and still feel hollow inside.

Because true transformation isn't about doing more—it's about being more aligned.

Inner Work Before Outer Wealth

Arup, before his rise, once tried to grow his business by mimicking a successful mentor. He used the same strategies, marketing words, and even wore similar clothes.

Yet it didn't work. Every time he spoke, something felt off—disconnected.

One evening, he broke down in front of his teacher, Guruji.

"Why do I sound fake even when I'm being sincere?"

Guruji, eyes calm like still water, responded,

"Because sincerity is not just about what you say—it's about what you *believe* when you say it. If your inner world doesn't match your outer action, the universe won't echo back what you seek."

The Bamboo's Secret

The Chinese bamboo tree doesn't break through the ground for the first five years. But it must be watered and cared for every single day.

When it finally sprouts, it can grow 90 feet in five weeks.

What was happening for those five years?

Root work.

Not visible, but vital.

Mindset is the *five years* beneath the surface that determines whether your breakthrough will last.

Without Mindset, Strategy Becomes...

- **Short-lived**: You'll burn out or self-sabotage.
- **Reactive**: You chase instead of create.
- **Conditional**: Your peace depends on performance.
- **Fragmented**: You live split between who you are and who you pretend to be.

With Aligned Mindset, Strategy Becomes...

- **Sustainable**: Because it's rooted in truth, not trend.
- **Authentic**: Because it's built on your essence, not ego.
- **Resilient**: Because failure refines, not defines you.
- **Magnetic**: Because energy—not effort—leads the way.

Reflection

Arup once wrote in his journal:

"I spent years chasing what I thought I wanted, only to realise I was not yet the man who could hold it."

"Now I tend to my roots more than my reach."

If you build a palace without a foundation, the first storm will humble you.

But if you build a strong inner world—anchored in clarity, presence, and belief—no storm can move you. In fact, you become the storm's teacher.

Journaling Prompt for the Reader:

Where am I applying strategy to fix what the mindset has left unresolved?

What version of me must rise internally before the external can match?

CHAPTER VI

Strategies of the Powerful and Wealthy

"The powerful don't just work hard—they build systems that keep working when they rest."

– Shree Shambav

Synopsis

Strategies of the Powerful and Wealthy pulls back the curtain on the playbook behind long-lasting influence and prosperity. This section breaks down the architecture of success—where vision isn't just a dream, but a map; where influence is cultivated intentionally, not by accident; and where positioning determines opportunity before talent is even seen. It explores how the wealthy and powerful build systems to escape the trap of trading time for money, and how they leverage strengths instead of spreading themselves thin. The power of proximity is revealed—mentorship, alliances, and silent partners who shift the tide behind the scenes. These strategies aren't reserved for the elite—they're replicable, if understood.

How Do Vision, Influence, and Strategic Positioning Work Together to Create Exponential Impact and Success?

Arup wasn't born into advantage. No legacy, no connections, no seed capital waiting in his name. But he was born with a

gaze—not outward toward what others had, but inward, to a flicker he couldn't ignore. That flicker was his **vision**.

Arup grew up in a quiet town where job security was everything and creativity was seen as a risk, not a gift. While his peers chased titles, Arup sat in cafés with notebooks, sketching out a dream of building a platform that would give village artisans global visibility—not just to sell their work, but to **preserve their soul**.

This was not a random idea. He had watched his own grandfather, die uncelebrated, his hands full of skill, his stomach often empty. Arup knew: **if the world could see them, it would value them.**

But **vision** alone couldn't feed the sculptors or scale the idea.

So he learned. Marketing. Technology. Storytelling. He travelled, spoke, failed, and rebuilt. But he didn't seek followers. He sought **to serve**—and that's when he began to gain **influence**.

Not the kind of influence built on viral tricks. This was slower. It came from **living the values he spoke of**. From paying fairly when no one was watching. From walking into boardrooms and refusing partnerships that compromised their dignity. People began to trust not just his idea—but **him**.

He became a reference point—not because he was loud, but because he was **true**.

But there was one more key that changed everything: **Strategic positioning**.

Arup realised early that posting artisan stories on social media wouldn't be enough. He needed **entry into luxury markets**, where perception shifted value. So, instead of launching his brand in crowded e-commerce spaces, he **curated a private gallery** in a metropolitan design district. Not because that was his background—but because that's **where attention met aspiration**.

The very same carvings once ignored at roadside stalls were now being discussed in interior design journals. Same product. Same people. **Different context.**

And suddenly—his small initiative became a **movement**.

The Triad in Motion

1. **Vision** gave Arup the *why*. It fuelled him through rejections and fatigue.

2. **Influence** gave him *trust*—not by power, but through authenticity.

3. **Strategic positioning** gave him *leverage*—by putting the right message in the right room.

This is the power of aligned intention.

Why It Matters to You

In your journey, you might already have a vision. You may even be trusted in small circles. But if you're not positioned where your gifts are **seen and needed**, your message will echo unheard.

Likewise, if you have influence but no vision, you'll be successful but hollow—driven by applause instead of purpose.

And if you have positioning without inner clarity or trust, people may see you—but they won't stay.

It is only when these three align—Vision, Influence, and Strategic Positioning—that your life becomes a force multiplier.

Not just a career. Not just wealth. But a **living legacy**.

You are not here to chase trends. You are here to **transmit light**—but to do that, the flame inside you must first be lit by vision, then magnified by influence, and finally, **aimed** through strategy.

Otherwise, you risk becoming a misplaced genius—burning brightly where no one needs your warmth.

But if you align them?

You don't just make waves.

You become the tide.

Would you like this expanded into a chapter, keynote, or illustrated framework for your book *The Silent Forces That Shape Destiny*?

Imagine a lighthouse.

Not just any lighthouse—but one built by a man, standing on a cliff edge that overlooks a volatile sea. He didn't build it because he was asked to. He built it because he saw something no one else did: ships—carrying dreams, people, goods—repeatedly crashing into the rocks, not for lack of strength, but for lack of **clarity**.

That lighthouse was his **vision**. Not just a building, but a symbol. A declaration. A whisper to the world: "You are not alone in the dark. There's a way."

But a vision, no matter how noble, means little if hidden.

So the man didn't stop at the structure. He lit the flame. And then he **amplified it**—not by shouting, but by **serving**. By listening to the sailors who survived. By learning the tides. By understanding when to shine brighter, and when to dim to avoid attracting the wrong ships.

This is where **influence** comes in.

Influence isn't manipulation. It's resonance. It's the ability to shape perception, not with noise, but with **truth lived so consistently that others begin to trust it instinctively**. Arup didn't force the sea to calm. He didn't control the winds. But he positioned himself in such a way that people began to navigate by his presence. He became a point of orientation.

And here's the key: **He didn't build his lighthouse in the middle of a desert.**

That is **strategic positioning**.

He understood that even the most radiant vision, and even the most trusted influence, will fade into obscurity if not placed where it matters. So he studied the maps. He chose the cliff.

He placed himself where his gifts intersected with the world's need—where visibility met utility.

He didn't just **have a vision**—he translated it into action.

He didn't just **want to help**—he earned the right to influence.

He didn't just **show up**—he showed up where he was needed most.

That's the holy trinity of exponential success:

1. **Vision** gives you the *why*.
2. **Influence** gives you the *reach*.
3. **Strategic positioning** gives you the *leverage*.

Without vision, you're successful but empty.

Without influence, you're brilliant but invisible.

Without a strategy, you're wise but ineffective.

And when all three align?

You don't just rise—you **elevate others in your wake**. Your life becomes a multiplier.

Real-World Reflection

Look at anyone whose impact reshaped culture—Mahatma Gandhi, Steve Jobs, Oprah Winfrey, Nelson Mandela.

- Gandhi had a **clear vision**: non-violent independence.

- He cultivated **massive influence** through sacrifice, consistency, and presence.

- He positioned himself **strategically**—not in government halls, but in salt marches, villages, and prison cells where his message couldn't be ignored.

Their rise wasn't accidental. It was **intentional orchestration of vision, influence, and placement.**

If you are clear on what you stand for, if you are willing to embody that with sincerity, and if you place yourself where you are most needed rather than most comfortable—then success is not a peak to chase.

It's a ripple you set in motion.

You become not just successful, but **significant**. Not just known, but **remembered**.

The world does not need more people screaming into the void.

It needs more lighthouses—rooted, radiant, and precisely placed.

That's how empires are built without shouting.

That's how destiny is not just shaped—but sculpted.

The Story of Karthik and the Garden of Systems

In a quiet village nestled between hills and rivers, Karthik stood before a plot of barren land. It stretched wide, sun-drenched but forgotten, its potential hidden beneath layers of neglect. While others rushed to plant fast crops in fertile valleys, chasing yield after yield with their sweat, Karthik did something curious.

He didn't plant right away.

He observed. He listened. He studied the sun's path, the way the rain kissed the soil, and how the winds caressed the edges. He noticed when the birds came, when the bugs swarmed, and when the silence spoke of fatigue. While others laboured daily under the hot sun, caught in cycles of toil and hope, Karthik worked differently. He wasn't just building a garden.

He was building a system.

Instead of one harvest, he envisioned a self-sustaining ecosystem—one that would feed itself, water itself, and protect itself. He dug a canal from the river that would flood the fields at sunrise. He planted trees whose fallen leaves became mulch for the soil. He attracted bees with fragrant flowers that doubled as medicinal herbs. He placed stones where water would pool, inviting birds to bathe, which would in turn fertilise the ground.

His neighbours laughed at first. "Too much thought, not enough action," they said.

But seasons passed.

And something remarkable happened.

While others still laboured daily for small gains, Karthik's garden bloomed—on its own. He had shifted from labourer to steward, from doer to designer. His time was now spent not in constant effort, but in refinement, innovation, and rest. He could mentor others, create new projects, and—most importantly—enjoy the life he had built.

The Hidden Machinery of the Powerful

Like Karthik's garden, the truly powerful and wealthy do not achieve freedom by doing more. They achieve it by building **systems** that grow their influence, wealth, and time **while they do less.**

These systems—often invisible to the untrained eye—are built on **three silent engines**:

Automation – The Mechanical Multiplier

Wealthy people do not trade time for money. They invest time in creating systems that **replace them.**

- In business, it's a sales funnel that works 24/7.
- In life, it's an optimised morning routine that removes decision fatigue.
- In communication, it's templated messages or content repurposed across platforms.

Automation is the bridge between human brilliance and technological leverage. It's what allows one person to speak to millions, one idea to ripple across continents, one effort to echo infinitely.

If you automate the right steps, your absence becomes more productive than your presence.

Delegation – The Trust Economy

True power isn't doing everything yourself. It's building a network of **competence and trust**.

From CEOs to artists, the wealthy surround themselves with those who are **better at specific tasks**—advisors, assistants, coaches, and creatives. They don't see asking for help as a weakness. They see it as wisdom.

Delegation frees the leader to **stay in their zone of genius**—to make high-impact decisions instead of drowning in low-leverage tasks.

Where others hoard control, the powerful extend trust—and in return, they multiply themselves.

3. Frameworks – The Wisdom That Repeats

Wealthy individuals don't reinvent the wheel. They build and follow **repeatable frameworks**—for decision-making, investing, hiring, scaling, and even relationships.

- They ask: What worked? What didn't? Why?
- They document, refine, and teach their methods.
- They make the invisible visible, so others can carry it forward.

These frameworks are **intellectual assets**—invisible yet invaluable. They turn chaotic effort into predictable progress.

A system isn't just a tool—it's a philosophy of living with clarity, precision, and intention.

The Illusion of Busyness vs. The Power of Structure

Karthik's neighbours were always tired. But they wore their exhaustion like a badge of honour. They equated motion with meaning, hustle with success. What they didn't see was that the wealthiest people were **not** the busiest—they were the most **strategic**.

Because **freedom is not earned through exhaustion—it is designed.**

We often believe we must work more to be more. But impact does not scale linearly with effort. It scales exponentially with leverage—when your systems, people, and wisdom carry your vision even while you sleep.

From Survival to Sovereignty

To move from reactive living to sovereign creation, one must pause the endless doing and ask:

- *What am I repeating that could be systemised?*
- *What am I doing alone that could be delegated?*
- *What wisdom do I need to capture so it works for me, again and again?*

This is not laziness. It is **elegance**.

Karthik didn't avoid work. He respected it so deeply that he built a system to honour it long after his hands stopped moving.

That is what the powerful do.

Build the Garden, Not Just the Harvest

You can toil for every grain, or you can build a garden that feeds you forever.

One is chasing.

The other is cultivating.

The world's most powerful are not always the smartest, richest, or most visible—they are the ones who quietly plant systems that outlive their labour, outgrow their effort, and outshine their presence.

So stop chasing output. Start building engines.

Let your life be like Karthik's garden: rooted in clarity, designed for ease, and flourishing without force.

Arup was not born to power. He was born to a quiet village nestled between the shoulders of forgotten hills. The village had no royalty, no legacy, no spotlight. Yet by the age of forty, Arup stood at the helm of an empire—not of land, but of minds, movements, and meaning.

People often asked, "How did you build this?"

They saw his speeches, his strategies, his rising name. What they did not see was the long corridor of silent doors that opened for him—doors he hadn't broken through with brute force, but doors whispered open by mentors, allies, and those who believed in him when he was nothing but a dream with a pulse.

This is the hidden reality of greatness.

Behind every visible success, there is an invisible architecture. A scaffolding of trust, wisdom, and belief that holds the weight until the structure can stand alone.

Let us walk that corridor with Arup—to see how the *uncarved throne* he eventually sat upon was shaped not just by his vision, but by the unseen hands of those who lifted him before the world even knew his name.

The Mentor: The Lighthouse Before the Storm

When Arup was sixteen, he met an old man named Gauran—an outcast mystic who lived in a hut outside the village.

Gauran never gave Arup direct answers. He gave him questions sharp enough to cut through delusion.

"What are you building—an image or a soul?"

Gauran didn't offer money or fame. He offered *clarity*—the most priceless resource at the beginning of any journey. He helped Arup see patterns, avoid self-sabotage, and prepare for storms not yet on the horizon.

Mentors are time-travellers.

They give you wisdom from futures you haven't lived yet. They save you from mistakes they've paid for with blood and heartbreak.

Without Gauran, Arup might've become brilliant—but bitter. Driven—but directionless.

The world celebrates the man on stage. It rarely sees the old man in the shadows who taught him how to speak.

The Allies: Builders of Bridges, Not Just Echoes

Years later, when Arup began to organise villages around cooperative development and educational reform, he encountered political resistance. Corrupt officials painted him as a threat. His movement stalled.

Then came Mira and Dev—two unlikely allies. She was a journalist with quiet power in urban circles. He was a logistics coordinator with influence on local unions. They saw the sincerity in Arup's cause and used their unique positions—not to take over, but to *amplify*.

Mira published stories that shaped public perception. Dev mobilised workers to distribute learning kits and safe food during the economic blockade.

These were not loud friendships. They were tactical *alliances*.

Allies don't just agree with your dream.

They stand in their lane and widen yours.

True alliances are sacred because they are not about *ownership*—they're about *orchestration*. Like a symphony where each plays a different instrument, but the same song.

Without Dev and Mira, Arup's voice would've been muffled. His idea would've lived—but not moved.

The Silent Backers: The Shadow Roots of the Great Trees

There came a time when Arup wanted to build a knowledge sanctuary—a place where thinkers, artists, scientists, and seekers could gather, away from noise and distraction. Land was scarce. Funds were tighter. Political roadblocks mounted.

And then, without fanfare, came a letter. Then another. Then a trustee offer. Three men and two women—none of whom wished to be named—stepped forward.

They were philanthropists, quiet titans in business and media. They had been watching Arup for years.

One wrote, *"The loudest people are not always the most worthy. But your silence echoes the truth. We invest not in what you promise, but in what you live."*

They provided seed funding, helped cut through bureaucracy, and never asked for credit. The sanctuary was built. It bore Arup's name. But its roots grew in their shadows.

Silent backers are not investors. They are spiritual shareholders.

They believe in impact over return. They sense future waves in present ripples.

Without them, Arup's sanctuary would've remained a sketch. With them, it became a sacred space for thousands.

The Unseen Architecture of Every Empire

In every empire—be it business, spiritual, artistic, or social—there are these three pillars that are often invisible:

1. **Mentorship** gives *depth and direction*.
2. **Alliances** provide *momentum and protection*.
3. **Silent backers** offer *resources and reach*.

When one is missing, the structure wobbles.

- Without mentors, you gain speed without wisdom.
- Without allies, you become a lone voice easily silenced.
- Without backers, you remain a candle without oil.

What makes these forces powerful is not just their presence—but their **purity**. These relationships are built not on transaction, but on *transcendence*—on shared purpose, mutual respect, and quiet alignment.

Real-World Reflections

- **Oprah Winfrey** was mentored by Maya Angelou, who gave her the confidence to carry her voice through cultural storms.
- **Steve Jobs** wasn't just a genius—he was backed by people like Mike Markkula, who shaped Apple's marketing DNA in silence.

- **Martin Luther King Jr.** had powerful allies like Bayard Rustin, who orchestrated behind-the-scenes strategy without ever taking public credit.

Their success looks solitary from the outside. But it was *crowded with angels*—some visible, some invisible.

The Kingdom Is Built in Quiet Rooms

The modern world glorifies independence. But **greatness is never solo.** It is carried, shaped, protected, and launched by unseen hands.

So if you dream of building something lasting:

- Seek not just followers, but **mentors.**
- Form not just friendships, but **alliances.**
- Attract not just applause, but **silent belief.**

Like Arup, your throne may one day be visible.

But remember—what allows you to sit on it is carved in quiet, by those who believed before anyone else could see.

And in time, **you too will become someone's unseen hand.**

That is how legacies are not just created—but passed on.

The River Knows Where to Flow

Why Leveraging One's Strengths Creates Asymmetrical Value

Arup stood at the edge of the mountain stream that carved through the forest behind his sanctuary. The water had been flowing for centuries—quiet, relentless, purposeful. It never tried to cover the entire forest. It never tried to move every rock. It chose a path. It deepened over time. And in doing so, it shaped valleys, fed crops, nourished life.

He watched it ripple and thought,

"The river does not waste itself trying to become rain, or ocean, or glacier. It becomes powerful by being itself—fully."

The Folly of Everything

In the early days of his journey, Arup fell for the myth of mastery.

He wanted to be everything: speaker, strategist, designer, coder, diplomat, philosopher, marketer. He believed that excellence was accumulation. To be great, he had to *know it all*.

He burned through nights learning tools he'd never use. He filled notebooks with plans that gathered dust. He diluted his presence chasing completeness.

And then, in a low season of exhaustion, Gauran visited him again. The old mentor placed a single seed in Arup's palm and said:

"This seed will never be a forest. But if it forgets to grow as itself, it will be nothing at all."

It struck him.

A mango tree doesn't bear coconuts. A hawk doesn't swim. The sun never apologises for not lighting the other side of the world.

Power comes not from *doing more*, but from *being truer*.

The Moment of Recognition

Arup sat with a blank parchment and drew three columns. At the top, he wrote:

- **Natural Flow**
- **Drains Me**
- **Neutral**

He realised that when he spoke, hearts stirred. When he listened, people opened. When he wrote, ideas sharpened like blades.

But when he tried managing logistics or navigating bureaucracy, his light dimmed. It wasn't that he was incapable—it's that he was misaligned.

And that's when the shift happened.

He stopped trying to become *a master of many*, and chose instead to become *a force in one*.

Focus Is Not Laziness. It's Precision.

The world romanticises the "polymath"—the genius who does everything. But most greatness is not built by doing *everything*. It's built by doing *one thing so deeply and authentically* that the ripple shakes other shores.

When Arup leaned into his strengths—public storytelling, deep listening, and unifying vision—his impact exploded. People *came to him*. Doors opened. Momentum became magnetic.

And here's what few realise:

When you shine in your zone of genius, others *want* to bring their genius to serve yours.

Asymmetrical Value: The Hidden Law of Greatness

A farmer can plant five crops and get five good yields. But if she finds the one that thrives best in her soil, her climate, her soul—and plants it with full devotion—she creates *surplus*. She now feeds not just herself, but the village.

That's asymmetrical value:

A focused strength, honed and scaled, can outperform scattered effort multiplied a hundred times.

Arup's decision to go all-in on what made him *uniquely* powerful didn't mean he ignored everything else. It meant he *delegated, partnered, or released* what dimmed his light.

He found Dev to build the logistics. Mira to carry his words into urban media. Priya is to structure the financials. He surrounded his depth with breadth.

He stopped trying to be the mountain—and became the spring.

How to Discover Your Strengths Like Arup Did

1. Notice What Feels Effortless but Powerful:
What do others thank you for? What leaves you energised instead of drained?

2. Pay Attention to What You Obsess Over in Silence:
Arup would lose hours writing, reflecting, speaking aloud to himself—not for show, but because it felt like breathing.

3. Study Your "Results to Effort" Ratio:

Where are you getting 80% of your results from 20% of your time? That's your strength calling.

4. Accept What You're Not Made For (Without Guilt):
When Arup let go of the need to be 'capable' in everything, he discovered freedom. And freedom is fuel for greatness.

Real-World Reflections

Steve Jobs wasn't an engineer. He was not great at coding. But he *saw*—he understood what humans would want before they knew it. He focused his energy on product design, experience, and vision. The rest, he delegated.

Serena Williams didn't try to become a world-class swimmer, violinist, or poet. She poured her soul into the court. Her strength had a name: **precision under pressure.**

Warren Buffett reads and reflects. That's his edge. He doesn't run the companies he invests in. He focuses on capital allocation—because *thinking clearly* is his deepest strength.

Arup's Reflection by the River

Years later, Arup's sanctuary was thriving. People studied there. Artists healed. Communities united. One student asked him,

"How did you do so much?"

Arup smiled.

"I didn't. I just did what I was meant to. And then, others brought their pieces to the puzzle."

He pointed at the river again.

"See how it flows? Not in every direction. Just one. But deep, relentless, and clear. That's what gives it the power to shape a valley."

The Lesson

You are not here to become everything.

You are here to become *something so fully, so purely,* that others see their path more clearly in your light.

Mastery is not knowing more.
It's being more of who you already are.

Let the river teach you.
Let Arup remind you.
Don't become the forest.
Become the tree that feeds it.

BORN TO RISE

CHAPTER VII

The Art of Compounding Everything

"What doesn't show up today might be growing roots beneath the surface. Compound wisely."

— Shree Shambav

Synopsis

The Art of Compounding Everything reveals the quiet magic that builds extraordinary lives—not through luck or bursts of genius, but through small, consistent actions repeated with intention. This section shows how compounding isn't just a financial strategy but a life philosophy. Whether it's deepening relationships, refining habits, or expanding knowledge, the invisible interest earned each day shapes tomorrow's realities. The 10-Year Rule challenges the reader to think long, act patiently, and build legacies, not just careers. The world often celebrates speed—but those who rise with depth, intention, and compounding wisdom outlast them all.

The Hidden Wealth of Time: The Unseen Compounding of Life

Arup once said to a young seeker in his sanctuary:

"What you water quietly each day becomes the forest others think grew overnight."

They were standing beside a Bodhi tree planted sixteen years ago—a thin sapling when Arup had arrived. Now, its wide canopy shaded scholars, monks, children, and tired travellers alike. The young seeker marvelled at its strength.

Arup smiled.

"The roots were growing when no one clapped."

The Shallow Vision: Why Most Never See It

In today's world of instant validation and 30-second wisdom, the principle of compounding has been stripped of its soul. It's become a financial cliché—charts of exponential growth, investment apps, and passive income dreams.

But money is the *smallest* thing that compounds.

The real wealth—the kind that builds unshakable character, deep love, vast wisdom, and spiritual grace—is grown quietly, invisibly, in places few ever look.

And because it is invisible at first—slow, unrewarded—it's overlooked.

Arup's Journey: The Seeds That Looked Like Nothing

In his twenties, Arup had nothing but a journal, a bookshelf, and a dream. He began waking up before dawn. Not to chase productivity, but to *centre himself*. Each morning, he read a few pages of ancient philosophy. He practised listening deeply. He wrote reflections, not for an audience, but for his soul.

At first, it changed nothing. No applause. No promotions. No miracles.

But *five years later*, his thoughts had depth that others didn't. His words carried the weight of stillness. His presence felt anchored, even in chaos. His insights pierced through the noise.

What seemed like "wisdom beyond his age" was nothing more than **invisible compound interest on sacred habits.**

1. Compounding Habits: The Brick That Becomes the Bridge

One brick laid today is meaningless. Ten thousand laid daily builds a bridge.

Arup didn't try to overhaul his life. He chose small rituals:

- One hour of deep reading each morning.
- One honest conversation per day.
- One small act of integrity, even when no one noticed.

Over time, these compounded into **inner architecture**. Not just results—but *resonance*.

Not just achievement—but *alignment*.

Great lives aren't built in sprints. They are *whispered into being*, one unseen choice at a time.

2. Compounding Relationships: The Echo of Trust

In a world of networking events and transactional friendships, Arup took a different path.

He showed up *consistently* for people.

- He sent thoughtful letters—without an agenda.//

- He remembered the small things—birthdays, losses, dreams shared in passing.

- He listened without interrupting, without trying to fix.

At first, it seemed like nothing.

Then, one day, when his village project faced sabotage, *people came*. Journalists, lawyers, donors, and village elders. Not out of obligation—but love.

The compounding of trust is quiet. But when it matures, it becomes **a fortress around your name.**

You can't buy it. You can't fake it. You earn it, brick by brick, smile by smile, year by year.

3. Compounding Knowledge: The Invisible Library Within

Arup never bragged about what he knew. He wasn't the loudest in a room. But when people asked hard questions, his answers felt *timeless*. Why?

Because he didn't just consume facts. He revisited ideas, let them mature, and wrestled with them over the years. He layered understanding like a slow-cooked meal.

The world values novelty. But wisdom values **integration**.

One book read ten times over ten years teaches more than ten books skimmed in one weekend.

Compounding knowledge is not information—it's **transformation over time**.

Why Most Miss It

Because in the beginning, compounding looks like *nothing*.

- You work out and see no change.
- You show kindness and they don't reciprocate.
- You study and still feel ignorant.

So most quit.

They chase bursts. Highs. Hacks.

But what they trade away is the slow magic that builds an *unshakable life force*.

The real miracle is not in what you do once, but in what you do daily even when no one claps.

The Bamboo That Sleeps

People see "overnight success." But it wasn't. It was **daily faith in invisible progress**.

Arup lived like a bamboo.

He grew downward before he grew upward.

The Sanctuary That Compounded

His sanctuary today hosts global thinkers, healers, and artists. It's not just a space—it's a *frequency*. But none of this was built with a big splash. It was:

- One conversation.
- One shared meal.
- One honest letter.
- One quiet prayer.
- Repeated over *decades*.

That's how the roots deepened. That's how the branches bore fruit.

Your Life: What Are You Compounding Today?

You may not see results today. But ask:

- What relationship are you showing up for daily?
- What truth are you nurturing in silence?
- What discipline are you repeating, not for applause—but for alignment?

Because when the season turns, when the sun hits the right angle—**everything you've planted will rise at once.**

And people will ask,

"How did you build this?"

You'll smile.

"Daily. Quietly. Through the years. When no one was watching."

The Final Whisper from Arup

"The world runs on flashes. But the soul grows in compounding."

Don't just invest your money.

Invest your minutes. Your mind. Your moments of grace.

Because in the end, the most valuable returns in life don't come from what you own.

They come from what you *honour daily*—in silence, in love, in presence.

That is the secret of the truly wealthy.

The Unseen Power of Consistency

"Arup," someone once asked him, "how did you do it? How did you become unstoppable?"

Arup looked out at the monsoon sky, its clouds dancing in unpredictable currents.

He simply said:

"I didn't outrun the storm. I outlasted it."

The Myth of the Grand Leap

The world romanticises transformation as something sudden. We talk of breakthroughs, viral moments, and strokes of genius.

But real progress is not a **burst**.

*It is a **beat**.*

A heartbeat.

A breath.

A quiet, repetitive devotion to the work that matters.

We think momentum is born from motivation.

But motivation is a spark.

Consistency is the firewood.

Arup and the Stone

In his youth, Arup visited a quarry on the edge of the forest where an old stonemason worked alone.

Every morning, the mason struck a massive boulder with a hammer. The first day: no crack. The fifth: nothing. The fiftieth: still the same.

But on the **101st strike**, the stone split in two.

Arup asked, "Was it the last strike that broke it?"

The mason replied:

"No. It was every strike. The last one just revealed it."

This stayed with Arup his entire life.

Because in a world obsessed with **events**, he learned to fall in love with **process**.

The Force that Ignores Mood and Moves Regardless

When Arup started his sanctuary, he committed to writing one letter every morning to a stranger, a donor, a volunteer, or a child. Rain or fever, celebration or sorrow—he wrote.

No reward. No feedback. Sometimes the letters were never read.

But one day, **one of those letters reached an ageing philosopher** in Paris, who then wrote about Arup's sanctuary. That article brought pilgrims, thinkers, and funding.

People called it lucky.

But luck visits those who show up every day—even when the path looks blank.

Why Consistency Builds Unstoppable Momentum?

Momentum isn't speed.

It's **direction multiplied by rhythm**.

The consistent person may seem slow at first—but over time, they become *un-catchable*. Why?

1. **They build systems, not whims.**

   When emotion dips, systems sustain.

   Arup didn't write when he felt inspired. He wrote because it was *Tuesday*.

2. **They create compound returns.**

   A 1% gain every day doesn't just add up. It *multiplies*.

   Consistency compounds trust, skills, and visibility.

3. **They master boredom.**

   Most quit because the path feels repetitive.

   But Arup found **sacredness in simplicity**—in doing small things with full presence.

How to Stay Consistent in Uncertainty: Arup's Practice

Even when the world was unpredictable—the economy unstable, projects sabotaged—Arup remained rooted. Here's how:

1. Anchor in Identity, Not Outcome

He never said, *"I want to build a sanctuary."*

He said, *"I am someone who serves learning."*

When your actions are tied to who you are, not what you achieve, you weather the storms of outcome.

2. Design Rituals, Not Resolutions

Arup created micro-rituals:

- A candle is lit before every planning session.
- A 10-minute tea ritual at sunrise to reset his mind.
- A 5-line gratitude note before sleep.

These were **anchors in chaos**. Small, unbreakable rhythms. Not grand plans that collapse under weight.

3. Accept the Imperfect Strike

Some days, his letter was uninspired. Some talks fell flat. Some efforts failed.

But he kept swinging.

Perfection paralyses.

Consistency liberates.

A dull blade used daily cuts deeper than a sharp one left in the drawer.

The River That Cut the Canyon

The Grand Canyon wasn't carved by a flood. It was carved by a **quiet river**, flowing daily for millions of years.

That river wasn't strong.

*It was **consistent.***

So it moved stone.

It rewrote geography.

It reshaped the face of the Earth.

You don't need to be brilliant.

You need to be **faithful to your rhythm.**

What Consistency Feels Like—and Why It's Hard

It feels boring. Repetitive. Thankless. Especially in the beginning.

You may:

- Show up and feel unnoticed.
- Practice and still feel behind.
- Serve and feel unappreciated.

But underneath that monotony, **roots are growing**. Deep and wide.

And when the season changes, everything will bloom at once.

Like Arup's tree. Like his sanctuary. Like the seeker he once was.

The Whisper Arup Leaves You With

"Don't chase the flood. Be the river."

"Don't wait for clarity. Be the candle."

"Don't pray for perfect days. Build your perfect rhythm."

One step.

Every day.

Through joy and sorrow.

Through noise and silence.

That is the true power behind any great soul. Not magic. Not talent.

But **holy repetition**.

Your Turn: What Is Your Small Strike Today?

- What daily habit feels small, but echoes of who you are becoming?
- What act of devotion can you repeat even when no one notices?
- What sacred rhythm can you keep, even in the rain?

Because one day, people will ask you, *"How did you become unstoppable?"*

And like Arup, you'll smile and say:

"I didn't move fast. I moved daily."

The 10-Year Rule: How Thinking in Decades Builds What Time Cannot Break

"Everyone wants transformation.

But few are willing to wait ten winters for a single bloom."

The Seed No One Watered

Arup was 24 when he first shared his dream of building a sanctuary of wisdom.

He was laughed at.

"Ten years? That's too long," they said. "The world moves faster now."

But Arup didn't flinch.

He smiled and planted his first seed anyway—not in soil, but in time.

He rented a broken warehouse and began cleaning it.

Alone.

With no money, no crowd, no applause.

But he wasn't thinking in **days**.

He was thinking in **decades**.

The Illusion of Urgency, The Truth of Time

We live in a world that worships speed.

- **30-day challenges**.

- **7-step hacks**.
- **Overnight virality**.

We confuse momentum with meaning.

But anything that rises overnight can vanish by morning.

Arup saw this. He had met many brilliant people whose empires collapsed because they were built on **reaction, not intention**.

"If it doesn't last, was it ever really a success?" he once asked.

The 10-Year Rule Defined.

The **10-Year Rule** is a quiet philosophy:

Whatever you want to be exceptional at, give it a decade of honest effort before judging the outcome.

Not ten days of excitement.

Not ten months of effort.

Ten **years** of intentional, iterative, patient pursuit.

It is a test: not of talent, but of **trust**.

In time. In process. In self.

What Thinking in Decades Does to You

1. It Burns Away the Shallow

When Arup stopped expecting quick returns, he also stopped chasing shallow ones.

He didn't build for applause—he built for alignment.

Short-term thinking is like planting plastic flowers.

They look good fast—but they're dead on arrival.

Thinking in decades forces you to choose work that truly matters.

Because you're going to live with it for a long time.

2. It Gives You the Patience of Mountains

In his fourth year, Arup's project nearly collapsed.

Funding dried up. Volunteers left. A storm destroyed half the building.

Someone asked, "Why not pivot to something else?"

He replied,

"If you quit every garden that hasn't bloomed in a year, you'll never taste your own fruit."

A decade-based vision helps you **hold still** when the winds howl.
Not because you're stubborn, but because you're rooted.

3. It Attracts the Right People

In year five, a quiet donor visited.

He had been silently watching Arup's work for years.

"I don't invest in noise," he said. "I invest in people who show up when the world isn't watching."

That is the truth:

Endurance filters allies from opportunists.

The longer you stay, the clearer your circle becomes.

The Bamboo That Waited

Was it growing fast then?

No. It was growing roots all along.

Arup's journey was just like that.

The world saw his rise. But his greatness was rooted in **invisible years**.

Why Most People Miss This Truth

Because the ego hates silence.

It wants immediate validation. It thrives on recognition.

But the soul?

The soul knows something deeper:

"Real power is not in what you build fast.

It's in what still stands after time has tried to tear it down."

What the 10-Year Rule Builds

- **Mastery** instead of mediocrity.

- **Legacy** instead of likes.

- **Endurance** instead of excitement.

Think of:

Vincent van Gogh – Art Born of Obscurity

Van Gogh sold **only one painting in his lifetime**.

He painted for nearly **a decade in poverty**, relentlessly exploring light, suffering, and beauty.

His work was dismissed, his mind doubted, yet he continued.

Now, his art is timeless.

Legacy was born not from approval, but from perseverance through invisibility.

Nelson Mandela – Freedom Forged in Time

Mandela spent **27 years in prison**, most of it in silence.

But those decades transformed a revolutionary into a statesman.

He emerged not bitter—but wise.

He led with grace, not vengeance.

The long arc of time gave him not just power—but the strength to wield it with peace.

Hayao Miyazaki – Decades Before Global Reverence

The founder of Studio Ghibli was drawing animations and obscure stories for **over 20 years** before "Spirited Away" won an Oscar.

Even then, he didn't chase fame—he chased **craft**.

His success bloomed after decades of storytelling, sketches, and silent belief in beauty.

Colonel Harland Sanders – The Late Bloomer

The founder of KFC was 65 when he began selling his recipe door-to-door.

Before that, he held over **a dozen odd jobs**, failed in multiple ventures, and slept in his car.

It took him **decades to refine his chicken recipe and pitch**—over 1,000 rejections.

His age didn't matter. His persistence did.

James Cameron – Years Beneath the Surface

Before *Titanic* or *Avatar*, Cameron spent **years studying deep-sea submersibles**, special effects, and story worlds.

Avatar took **almost a decade** to conceptualise and create.

He wasn't just building a film. He was building a world that would outlive hype.

Vera Wang – Reinvented at 40

Vera Wang was a **figure skater, then a journalist** before she ever touched bridal fashion.

She entered the design world **at age 40**, with no formal background.

Now, her name defines an entire industry.

Reinvention + Long View = Timeless Impact.

Malcolm Gladwell's 10,000 Hours

His principle: It takes **10,000 hours** of deliberate practice to achieve world-class mastery in any field.

Ten years of daily practice = 10,000 hours.

Whether you're a violinist or a visionary—the timeline still applies.

How to Live This Principle:

1. Choose What You Can Love in Silence

Before the world claps, will you still care for this dream?

Arup used to say, *"If you can love it in the dark, it will shine in the light."*

2. Document, Don't Demand

Every month, Arup would write a reflection—what worked, what failed, what he learned.

He didn't measure his worth by wins—but by **witnessing his own evolution**.

3. Redefine Progress

Instead of asking, *"How far am I?"*

He asked, *"How deep am I?"*

Because progress in the long game is not forward—it is **inward**.

The Whisper Arup Leaves Behind

One evening, at a gathering of young dreamers, someone asked:

"What if I give 10 years and still fail?"

Arup smiled gently and said:

"You won't fail. You will **become**."

And what you become will outlast any success you were chasing."

A Final Reflection for You

What would you still build if it took ten years?

What dream would still be worth your time if no one clapped until the end?

Because those are the ones that will leave fingerprints on eternity.

Think in decades—not days.

And like Arup, you may one day sit in a garden you planted long ago, blooming at last, knowing that your patience became your power.

The Echo Beyond the Hills: How Compounding Builds Legacy

Arup stood barefoot in the courtyard of the sanctuary he had built—not with marble, but with meaning.

Children ran between banyan trees, elders read under the arches, and somewhere in the far meditation hall, a young woman was reciting poetry written before she was born.

She didn't know it, but the words she spoke were seeded by Arup thirty years ago.

Not written.

Seeded.

Because that's how legacy grows—not as content, but as *compounding intention*.

The Wells We May Never Drink From

When Arup was young, he once helped an old man named Hari dig a well in their village. The sun was cruel. The soil was stubborn.

After two weeks of toil, Arup said, "Why are we digging here? There's no sign of water."

Hari smiled. "We're not digging for water. We're digging for the child who'll need it when we're gone."

Years later, a drought came.

That well saved three families.

Arup remembered.

That was the first time he understood the **difference between impact and legacy**:

- **Impact** is what you do *that is seen*.
- **Legacy** is what you do *that becomes unseen—but continues*.

Legacy is the forest grown from a single acorn, long after the hand that planted it has turned to dust.

The Nature of True Compounding

Most people hear "compounding" and think of **money**. But that's only the smallest form.

The deepest compounding happens in three invisible dimensions:

1. In Values

Every time you choose honesty over convenience,

Every time you speak truth with love instead of silence with fear,

Every time you model integrity when no one watches—

You are compounding your **character**.

And that character shapes how your children will make decisions.

How your employees will lead?

How your partners will trust?

Values compound not in results—but in the culture you leave behind.

2. In Relationships

Every moment of patient listening, every letter written, every grudge forgiven—

These are not wasted gestures. They are **investments in relational capital**.

Your kindness will teach someone how to treat others.

Your mentorship will ripple into the next mentor.

Your loyalty will become someone's blueprint for love.

Relationships compound across generations through emotional DNA.

3. In Wisdom

Books read.

Mistakes journaled.

Stories passed down.

Every ounce of wisdom you gain but don't hoard becomes a **compound library** for someone else.

When Arup finally wrote his reflections—not to impress, but to preserve—his daughter read them.

She passed them to a young teacher.

The teacher built a curriculum that now shapes many students.

All from one quiet evening when Arup chose to write instead of scroll.

Knowledge compounds when it's shared across time, not just across timelines.

Challenging the Age of Now

The modern world sells you urgency:

- Go viral now.
- Monetise fast.
- Post, pivot, repeat.

But legacy whispers a different truth:

"Do what matters, even when it's invisible. Especially when it's invisible."

Because the things that shape eternity rarely trend.

Aligning Today With Tomorrow's Grandchildren

To live in alignment with legacy is to see yourself not as the hero of the story—but the soil.

It's to ask:

- "Will this decision nourish those I will never meet?"
- "Does my schedule today serve only my survival—or someone else's future strength?"
- "If someone found my diary a hundred years from now, would they find truth, or noise?"

When Arup built the knowledge sanctuary, he planted a grove of sandalwood trees nearby. They take 15 to 20 years to mature.

He told a visitor, "These are not for me. They're for the children of the children who come here."

Legacy is Not a Monument. It's a Mural

You don't have to be famous to leave a legacy.

You just need to:

- Live by principle even when it's slow.
- Teach the next with more generosity than you were taught.
- Build systems that outlive you: journals, rituals, libraries, gardens, foundations, practices.

The man who plants trees whose shade he will never sit under—is the one who understands legacy.

Reflection: The River and the Raindrop

We are not the river.

We are the **raindrops** that feed it.

But every raindrop, consistent and quiet, becomes part of a current that one day carves canyons, feeds cities, and nourishes generations.

Live as a conscious raindrop.

Your quiet actions today may become someone's river tomorrow.

That is the miracle of compounding.

That is the soul of legacy.

CHAPTER VIII

The Psychology of Money

"You don't just earn money—you inherit beliefs about it. Heal the belief, change the outcome."

– Shree Shambav

Synopsis

The Psychology of Money dives beneath the surface of bank balances and income streams to reveal the hidden emotional forces that govern financial lives. More than a tool, money is an emotional symbol—often tangled in fear, guilt, shame, or pride. This section illuminates how early experiences, family narratives, and societal conditioning shape our relationship with money, usually unconsciously. But it also offers a path to healing. By understanding money as energy and addressing emotional wounds, readers are empowered to rewrite their financial story—not just through smarter choices, but through inner transformation. When the psychology shifts, the reality often follows.

The Shadows Beneath the Ledger

Arup sat across the table from a young entrepreneur—clever, visionary, and broke.

The man had launched three ventures. Each had a promise. Each had failed.

Not from lack of skill.

But something deeper. Quieter. Like a shadow just beyond the lamp's reach.

"I don't know what's wrong with me," the man confessed. "Every time I start to succeed, I pull back. I delay. I overthink. I shrink."

Arup didn't offer advice. He offered silence.

Then he asked, "When you were growing up, what did your family say about money?"

The man chuckled nervously. "That rich people were greedy. That money ruins relationships. That wanting too much is selfish."

And there it was.

Not a strategy problem.

A **subconscious loyalty to struggle**.

The Emotional Currency of Money

Money is not just a number.

It is **an emotional container**.

Each rupee, each dollar, each decision—holds within it an echo of our earliest feelings: of **safety, shame, scarcity,** or **significance.**

And three of the most powerful emotional forces that distort our financial lives are:

1. Fear: The Silent Accountant

Fear is primal. It tells us, **"There's not enough."**

Not enough money. Not enough time. Not enough worth.

It leads to hoarding. Or hesitation. Or hustle without peace.

Arup remembered his own past. The lean years in his village. His mother stretching coins like dough. Fear taught him to survive—but it nearly kept him from **expanding**.

He once turned down a high-potential opportunity simply because **it felt too big**—and therefore dangerous.

Fear whispers: "Stay small. Stay safe."

But here's the truth:

Fear is a fog, not a fact.

It distorts vision but holds no substance once walked through.

The antidote?

Clarity and courage.

Ask yourself not what you fear will happen—but what you fear will awaken within you if it does.

2. Guilt: The Hidden Tax

Guilt says, "You don't deserve this."

It sneaks in when money flows easily. When abundance knocks gently.

Especially for those from humble roots—when earning more than your parents ever did in a month, in a single hour—it can feel like betrayal.

So we unconsciously sabotage:

- Overspending what we earn.
- Undercharging for what we give.
- Giving too much, too often, with resentment hidden beneath generosity.

But guilt doesn't come from prosperity. It comes from **conditioning**—from believing that worth is tied to suffering.

Arup once gave away 90% of an award fund he received, not out of charity, but out of discomfort.

He had to learn:

You don't honour your past by staying in its cage.

You honour it by breaking its ceiling—and building others a ladder.

3. Greed: The Thirst That Never Ends

Greed is not always loud.

Sometimes, it looks like an achievement.
Like "more" that never ends.

It's the constant climb that ignores rest.
The chase that forgets to ask, "Why?"

Greed comes when money is mistaken for meaning.
When we use it to fill emotional voids, it was never designed to satisfy.

Arup saw this in a business magnate who never spent his wealth—but couldn't stop accumulating.

"You're not building a fortune," Arup told him. *"You're building a wall around a wound."*

The medicine?

Sufficiency and purpose.

Knowing when enough is truly enough—and why we're gathering what we do.

The Subconscious Ledger

What drives your financial life isn't your spreadsheet.

It's your **emotional ledger**—formed by:

- The stories you heard.
- The behaviours you watched.

- The conclusions your young self drew when no one explained otherwise.

If you were taught that asking for money was rude,

or that poverty equals purity,

or that rich people are corrupt…

…you will unconsciously make decisions to stay "morally safe,"

even if that safety comes with chains.

The Reframe: From Scarcity to Sovereignty

To heal your relationship with money, you must **re-parent the parts of you that relate to it emotionally**.

Here's how:

1. Awareness is the First Currency

Write your early money memories.

What did your parents say about wealth, bills, debt, and ambition?

Identify the emotional charge. Is it fear? Shame? Pride? Anger?

Naming the ghost is the first step to freeing yourself from it.

2. Redefine Deserving

You are not bad for wanting more.

You are not wrong for succeeding.

You are not disloyal to your past if you grow beyond it.

You were not born to repeat scarcity.

You were born to **transform it into strength.**

3. Anchor Money to Meaning

When your money is in service of something deeper—

A cause, a community, a calling—

You'll spend and earn with cleaner energy.

Greed fades when meaning rises.

Fear shrinks when purpose expands.

Guilt dissolves when aligned with generosity without martyrdom.

The Legacy of Financial Freedom

Arup's story was not about building wealth.

It was about **healing his inner economy** first.

Once he did, he could lead others not just in earning more—

But in **liberating more.**

Wealth, in its truest form, is not stored in banks.

It is stored in your nervous system, your decisions, and your values.

So ask yourself:

"What emotion is driving my financial life today?

And what new story am I ready to live, starting now?"

Because the day you shift your internal currency—

The world begins to pay you in ways that last.

The Mirror That Counts

In a quiet temple town, not far from the rush of commerce, lived an old potter named Veeran.

He had never seen much wealth, yet people came to him for more than his clay pots. They came for wisdom. For stillness. For clarity.

One day, a young man named Vishal, torn between ambition and confusion, visited him.

"I don't understand," Vishal said, placing his branded laptop bag carefully on the dusty floor. "I've done everything right. Built my startup. Grown a team. But money feels… heavy. It flows in, but it disappears. And even when it stays, I feel anxious—like I'm holding something I haven't earned."

Veeran smiled and handed him a cracked pot.

"What do you see?"

Vishal looked. "A broken pot."

"No," said Veeran. "A reflection of your mind. Money is the same. It doesn't change your essence. It simply **reveals your fractures.**"

Money Is Not Just Currency. It Is a Mirror.

Money is **energy made visible**. A sacred contract we've assigned value to—but its true significance is far beyond economics.

In truth:

- Money reflects our **self-worth**: What we believe we deserve—not what we say we want.

- It mirrors our **relationships**: How we give, receive, trust, or withhold.

- And it echoes our **internal alignment**: Whether our soul, mind, and heart are working in harmony—or quietly at war.

1. Self-Worth: The First Vault

What you earn is not just about your skill—it is about what you **feel worthy of receiving.**

A brilliant woman might undercharge for her services not because she lacks ability, but because deep inside, she was taught:

"Good girls don't ask for too much."

"Nice people don't focus on money."

"Your value lies in sacrifice."

So every time she sends an invoice, her hands tremble with invisible shame.

You see, money has no opinion.

It simply responds to the energy with which it is welcomed or resisted.

If you subconsciously believe you are not enough, money will behave accordingly.

It will flee, avoid, or sabotage itself—until your self-worth is recalibrated.

Self-worth is the vault.

Money is just what's allowed to enter.

2. Relationships: The Flow of Giving and Receiving

How you handle money is often a reflection of how you **handle people.**

- Are you generous, but secretly resentful?

You might be giving from guilt, not love.

- Are you always receiving but feel like a burden?

You may be carrying hidden beliefs about your lack of contribution.

- Are you tight-fisted, even with yourself?

You might be projecting trust issues onto money.

Money mimics the energy of your relationships.

If you treat yourself with respect, you spend and invest differently.

If you trust life, you allow money to flow in and out with grace.

Vishal once realised he was hoarding money not for safety—but because he feared abandonment. Just like his father once left without a goodbye.

Money had become **the substitute for love**.

When he healed that wound, money flowed with less friction—because he no longer expected it to fix what only forgiveness could.

3. Internal Energy: Alignment and Integrity

Have you ever made money and still felt... hollow?

That's because money earned out of alignment—

Out of deceit, desperation, or ego—

Carries the residue of its origin.

You may buy it, but never feel nourished.

True wealth is not accumulation. It is **alignment.**

When your inner values and your outer income match, there is peace. There is pride. There is power.

The artist who sells one honest painting may feel richer than the executive who earns millions selling his soul.

Because one sleeps in **truth**. The other, in **transaction.**

The Sacred Exchange

Money is not evil.

Nor is it holy.

It is **neutral—but not numb**.

It **records your emotional frequency** like a diary.

Every expense is a vote for what you value.

Every earning is a reflection of what you believe you're worthy of.

Every act of giving or receiving is a spiritual act.

To align with money deeply, ask:

- Do I respect where it comes from?
- Do I trust how I use it?
- Do I allow it to support—not define—me?

The Return to Wholeness

Veeran gave Vishal a final teaching before he left:

"Fill the pot," he said, pointing to the cracked one.

"But it leaks," Vishal protested.

"Exactly. And so does your life, if your soul is fractured. Fix the pot—not by tape, but by **truth**. And the water, like money, will stay where it is meant to."

Vishal didn't become rich overnight.

But he began to **earn without apology**,

spend with clarity,

and give with peace.

In time, money became not his master, nor his identity—

but his **mirror**,

reflecting back the light he carried within.

Reflection

1. What emotional patterns from childhood still dictate your relationship with money?
2. In what areas of your life do you feel "underpaid"—and is that tied to your self-worth?
3. Are you using money to cover emotional wounds that require inner healing?
4. If money could talk, what would it say about the way you treat yourself?

Final Thought:

"Money doesn't make you who you are.

It shows you who you've been—

And invites you to choose who you wish to become."

"More Than Paper: The Inner Myths of Money"

The Currency of the Soul

Money, in its rawest form, is neutral—just inked paper, digital digits, or coins cast in metal. But to the human mind and heart, money is never just that.

It becomes a **symbol, myth, mirror,** and **identity.**

We don't live by the numbers in our accounts.

We live by the *narratives* we've attached to those numbers.

What Money *Represents* (Unconsciously)

Let's uncover what money symbolises in the unconscious mind—and how these symbols shape destiny.

1. Money as Love

"If I have more, they'll stay. If I don't, I'll be left."

Many people, especially those who experienced emotional abandonment, unconsciously equate money with **connection and approval.**

The belief:

"If I'm financially successful, I will be seen. I'll be valued. I'll be loved."

This leads to:

- Overgiving to please others
- Undercharging to avoid rejection
- Obsessive earning to prove worth

But when money becomes a proxy for love, we confuse **transaction** with **affection**—and end up feeling emotionally bankrupt even when financially stable.

2. Money as Power or Safety

"When I have money, I'm untouchable. When I don't, I'm invisible."

Those who grew up in chaotic or unsafe environments often view money as the **only barrier** between them and danger, disrespect, or dependency.

They may:

- Hoard money with tight fists
- Over-control every expense
- Struggle to trust partners or collaborators

The belief:

"Money = control. Without it, I'm vulnerable."

But this mindset often blocks the flow of abundance. Fear-driven money tends to stagnate—it becomes a **fortress**, not a **flow**.

3. Money as Identity

"My bank balance determines my self-worth."

In a society that glorifies wealth, many internalise the myth that **net worth = personal worth**.

This fuels:

- Shame during financial struggle
- Arrogance during financial success

- Emotional volatility tied to money wins or losses

It traps the soul in a seesaw:

"If I lose money, I'm a failure."

"If I make money, I'm superior."

This belief leads to fragile self-esteem and burnout. Because when **your worth depends on what you have**, you never truly rest—you only chase.

4. Money as Guilt or Sin

"Having too much is selfish." "Rich people are bad."

For many, especially in spiritual or modest backgrounds, money is unconsciously linked to **moral compromise**.

- "It's wrong to want more."
- "If I'm wealthy, I must be hurting someone else."
- "Spiritual people don't focus on money."

This narrative causes self-sabotage:

They reject wealth even when it's within reach.

They feel guilt while receiving.

They shrink when opportunities arise.

The result? Constant push-pull energy with money. Wanting it, then repelling it.

5. Money as Scarcity (or Trauma Echo)

"There's never enough."

Those shaped by poverty, financial trauma, or ancestral scarcity may carry **deep, cellular fear** around money—even when circumstances improve.

This fear manifests as:

- Compulsive saving or overspending
- Under investing in personal growth
- Distrust in abundance

They live as if wealth is a fleeting flame—One misstep and it's gone.

The problem? **They can't fully enjoy or expand what they have.**

Because the nervous system is stuck in survival mode.

The Stories We Carry—And the Lives They Shape

Every belief becomes a script.

Every script becomes a pattern.

Over time, we don't just spend money.

We **perform it**—enacting the same unconscious roles again and again.

- The Martyr ("I don't need much. I'll just give it away.")

- The Hero ("I'll rescue everyone. I'll fix the family with money.")

- The Rebel ("I don't care about money. It's all corrupt.")

- The Chaser ("Once I make *this* amount, then I'll be happy.")

And underneath them all?

A child waiting to be seen.

A wound waiting to be healed.

A belief waiting to be rewritten.

From Symbol to Sacred Stewardship

To change our financial reality, we must stop obsessing over **money itself**—and start healing what it **represents.**

How?

- **Journal your Money Story**:

What did your parents teach you about money?

What emotions come up when you think of wealth?

- **Disentangle Money from Identity**:

Practice seeing yourself as whole regardless of income.

- **Bless Your Earnings and Spendings**:

Turn every financial act into a conscious ritual of gratitude and growth.

- **Invest in Alignment, Not Appearance**:

Let money serve your soul's truth, not your ego's hunger.

- **Forgive the Past**:

Money trauma is real—but healing is possible.

You are allowed to write a new chapter.

Reflection

"Money is not the destination.

It is the reflection of your journey."

— *Shree Shambav*

When you clear the distortions in your beliefs,

When you replace shame with sovereignty,

When you treat money not as a god or a villain,

But as **a mirror for your healing**—

Then you no longer chase it.

You attract it.

You grow it—with grace.

And you give it—

From a place of wholeness, not woundedness.

The Inheritance We Don't See

The Shadow Ledger

In a quiet town wrapped between mountains and mango groves, a woman named Olivia sat at her kitchen table late at night—again—staring at her monthly bank statement, her jaw clenched, stomach tight, heart heavy. The numbers were never just numbers. They were echoes. Ghosts.

As a child, Olivia had watched her father come home bone-tired, hands rough from construction, barely speaking a word. Every rupee was rationed like breath. Her mother kept money in an old rice tin above the fridge, hidden—not just from thieves, but from hope itself.

In Olivia's world, money wasn't a tool.

It was a *threat*.

It disappeared. It disappointed.

It made people fight.

It made her feel… small.

So now, even as a grown woman with a steady job and a decent income, Olivia felt guilt every time she spent on herself. She undercharged for her services. She gave too much. She feared checking her bank balance. Not because she was broke—but because **she didn't feel worthy of abundance.**

The ledger she carried wasn't just financial.

It was emotional.

It was ancestral.

What We Inherit Without Realising

Most of us carry **two kinds of inheritances:**

1. **The visible** – money, land, debt, savings
2. **The invisible** – beliefs, fears, patterns, shame

And the second often matters more.

You may not have inherited your father's watch, but you may have inherited his fear of risk. You may not have received a trust fund, but you may have inherited your grandmother's guilt over wanting nice things.

You may not even remember the exact stories—but they live in you, in whispers like:

- "I must work twice as hard to deserve."
- "There's never enough."
- "Wanting more is selfish."
- "I'm not good with money."

These beliefs become your *baseline operating system*. Until you rewrite them, they'll quietly run the show.

The Path to Financial Healing: From Scarcity to Sovereignty

So, how do we begin?

1. Acknowledge the Wound Without Shame

You can't heal what you won't face.

Like any trauma, financial wounds need naming. Sit with your story. Write it out. Cry if you need to. Ask:

- What did money mean in my childhood?
- What messages did I receive about wealth, poverty, worth?
- Who did I see suffer because of money?
- Who did I see control others through it?

Your money mindset was **not your fault.**

But it **is now your responsibility.**

This is not blame. This is *power reclamation.*

2. Separate Self-Worth from Net Worth

You are not your balance sheet.

You are not your savings, your salary, your credit score.

Start saying:

"I am inherently worthy of ease, rest, and abundance."

"Money is not a measure of my soul."

"I can be enough and still grow."

Money can amplify your life, but it cannot define your value. Your **true worth** is eternal—it is soul-deep, not spreadsheet-deep.

3. Rewrite the Inner Script

"If your mind is the soil, your beliefs are the seeds. Choose them with care."

Use conscious affirmations not as empty slogans, but as emotional re-scripting. Examples:

- "Wealth flows to me when I am aligned with truth."
- "I spend with love. I receive with openness."
- "I deserve financial peace, not just survival."

And more importantly, **act** in accordance with the new belief—even in small ways:

- Invest in your learning.
- Raise your prices.
- Say no to energy-draining favours.
- Track your income with gratitude, not dread.

4. Forgive the Past (Even If You Can't Forget It)

Forgive your younger self—for overspending, for staying silent, for not knowing better.

Forgive your parents—for passing down fears instead of abundance.

They did what they could with what they had.

"Financial healing is not about changing the past.

It's about ending the loop."

When you forgive, you **break the chain**. You no longer carry scarcity as inheritance—you plant wealth as legacy.

5. Build New Emotional Associations With Money

If your nervous system has linked money with fear, guilt, or shame, it's time to *rewire*.

Do this through **ritual and repetition**:

- Bless your wallet.
- Say thank you when paying bills.
- Light a candle when receiving payment.
- Celebrate small wins.
- Save and give joyfully.

Make money a **sacred ally**, not a source of anxiety. Show your system: *"This is safe. This is good. This is love in motion."*

6. Focus on Contribution, Not Just Accumulation

True financial power comes when you see money not just as *what you keep*, but as *what you enable*.

Ask:

- "How can I let money magnify my gifts?"
- "How can I use money to heal, help, build, uplift?"

Money earned through alignment and used with intention becomes **spiritual currency.**

It doesn't just buy—it **blesses.**

A Legacy Rewritten

Back in that mountain town, Olivia eventually began to heal. Not overnight. But steadily.

She created a "money altar" with stones and affirmations.

She started charging her true worth.

She stopped apologising for wanting more.

She even opened an account for her niece's education.

"Let her know," Olivia whispered, "that we are no longer afraid of money."

Her family didn't understand at first.

But they felt the shift.

Because when even *one person heals*, generations begin to rise.

Reflection: From Wound to Wealth

"You are not just healing your bank account.

You are healing the belief that you were ever not enough."

This journey isn't just about getting rich.

It's about **becoming whole.**

Because a healed relationship with money is not loud.

It's quiet, rooted, generous, and strong.

It's no longer about proving.

It's about *creating*.

For yourself.

For your children.

For those whose names you'll never know—but whose lives you'll touch, because *you chose to heal*.

WRAP UP

The Sacred Pause

"When power is guided by purpose and riches are shaped by values, a life of legacy begins to unfold."

— Shree Shambav

Synopsis

As this journey of clarity and mindset draws to a close, a deeper question emerges: What are you truly seeking—status, security, or soulful significance? This section invites you to pause, reflect, and recalibrate your inner compass. Power and wealth are no longer external pursuits alone, but reflections of your internal alignment. True success asks not just what you have, but who you are becoming through it. Before rising higher, you are asked to rise truer—toward a life where ambition meets purpose and prosperity meets peace.

The Mirror Behind the Mountain

What Are You Truly Seeking?

There comes a moment in every climb when the summit disappears behind the clouds, and the only thing left to confront is the self.

You've walked through the terrain—clarity sharpened like a blade, mindset forged in fires of ambition. You've studied power not just as dominance, but as direction. You've defined riches not merely as numbers, but as capacity. You've explored wealth not only as possession, but as possibility.

But now, at the edge of Part One, as the horizon of your life widens, a more haunting, more honest question arises—not of what you want, but why you want it.

What are you truly seeking?

Not the shiny surface answer. But the sacred, inner cry that echoes in quiet moments when no one's watching. Is it really power you want—or the **freedom** it might buy? Is it riches—or the **impact** you imagine it could fund? Is it wealth—or the **inner peace** you hope it will finally give you permission to feel?

This is the turning point most never reach, because the outer world rewards motion, not meaning.

But you're not "most people," are you?

The Mirror Merchant

Long ago, in a sun-drenched village nestled between two mountain ranges, there lived a mirror merchant named Kaviraj. He was known far and wide for crafting the clearest, most flawless mirrors—mirrors that princes and priests would travel for days to purchase.

He grew wealthy. Very wealthy.

One day, an old traveller came to him—not to buy, but to offer. He carried a dusty, cracked, uneven piece of reflective glass.

"This is the most important mirror you'll ever hold," the traveller said.

Kaviraj laughed. "I sell mirrors better than this to kings."

The traveller nodded, "Yes, but none of your mirrors show you what this one can: **your soul behind your success.**"

Years passed. Kaviraj's business thrived. But so did a quiet ache. Late at night, when he was alone, he would stare into that old mirror. And slowly, painfully, beautifully—he began to see beyond his wealth.

He saw his longing for his father's approval. His fear of irrelevance. His hidden desire was not to be admired, but to be **loved for who he was without the empire.**

It broke him. But it also built him.

Eventually, Kaviraj stopped selling mirrors. He began teaching young seekers to craft them—not just of glass, but of consciousness. His fortune faded. His fame did not. But his peace—*his peace was finally his own.*

Inherited Dreams or Inner Desires?

Too many of us chase dreams that aren't our own—scripts handed down by well-meaning parents, success models shaped by societal applause, ambitions born from insecurity rather than insight.

We mistake motion for meaning. We gather followers but lose our centre. We accumulate without anchoring.

But true power, true riches, true wealth—*they expand you*, they don't consume you.

So here's your real task:

Strip your pursuit down to its essence.

Ask, again and again:

"Is this mine, or was it given to me without my conscious consent?"

"Does this goal bring me closer to wholeness or just closer to applause?"

Because here's the truth:

- Power without purpose becomes control.
- Riches without resonance become noise.
- Wealth without wisdom becomes weight.

But when these are aligned with your soul's architecture, they become portals—into freedom, into grace, into a life that not only looks successful but **feels sacred.**

The Inner Compass for the Next Climb

You've built the base. You've understood the terrain. You've met the voices inside you—the driven one, the doubter, the dreamer.

Now, before we transition into the next season of this journey—*from mastery to meaning*—you must bring your compass home.

Recalibrate it not to inherit Norths, but to **your own inner star.**

Let this question not be an end, but an invitation:

"Am I building a life that is **true**, not just triumphant? One that I would choose again—even if no one ever saw it?"

Let that question echo. Let it haunt you beautifully. Let it free you.

Because when your **desires are yours**, and your **success is soulful**,

then—and only then—your rise will never need to end.

The Currency of the Unseen

Has Your Definition of Wealth Evolved to Include Not Just Assets, But Awareness?

In the beginning, wealth feels simple.

It is the house on the hill. The account that never empties. The schedule that bends to your will. It is numbers, status, comfort—the visible trophies of achievement.

But then the climb begins. The grind sharpens your mind, yes—but it also begins to hollow out your soul if you're not careful. And slowly, the questions arrive. Soft at first. Then urgent. Then undeniable.

What if **real wealth** isn't just what you *accumulate*—but what you *awaken*?

What if the richest among us are not always those with the largest estates... but those whose inner landscape is fertile with meaning, stillness, and deep presence?

Aranya's Garden

There was once a wealthy landowner named Aranya who had everything—gold, servants, estates that stretched beyond the eye's horizon. But at night, he couldn't sleep. His heart raced with fear of loss. His mind was always planning, protecting, and defending.

One day, weary from his own abundance, he met a gardener named Maitreyi who lived in a modest hut outside the city walls. She had a tiny patch of land, barely enough to feed her. But her eyes sparkled with a joy that Aranya had not known in years.

"Why are you so happy?" Aranya asked, genuinely perplexed.

Maitreyi smiled. "Because I tend to the **garden inside me** every day. And it grows richer, even when my pantry does not."

Moved by her peace, Aranya began to visit. She taught him silence. Presence. Gratitude. The beauty of watching a single rose bloom. Over time, he started spending less time in his boardrooms and more in her garden.

When he died decades later, his will shocked everyone. He left behind not just his riches—but a letter that read:

"I was once a man who owned everything and felt nothing.

Then I met someone who owned little, but felt everything.

That was the day I began to truly live.

And *that* was the day I became wealthy."

Beyond Assets: The Awakening

This journey—yours, mine, ours—is not just about acquiring more. It's about *becoming more.*

- Awareness is a currency no market can trade.

- Presence is a luxury no fortune can fake.

- A clear conscience is a soft pillow no gold can replace.

True wealth is when your outer world reflects the peace of your inner one. When your success doesn't cost your soul. When your time belongs to what you value. When your heart is not collateral damage in the pursuit of progress.

Wealth, when evolved, becomes **invisible capital**:

The depth of your listening.

The lightness of your being.

The strength of your character.

The joy in your giving.

The calm in your solitude.

The Redefinition of Rich

So, pause for a moment.

Has this journey—through clarity, mindset, and unspoken principles—reshaped your view of what it means to be truly rich?

- Can you feel the shift from *having* to *being*?

- From seeking validation to living in alignment?

- From external wealth to *embodied* wealth?

Because that shift—that quiet, seismic shift—is the very threshold between Book One and what lies ahead.

This Is the New Rich

Let this be your new benchmark:

"I am rich not just because of what I've earned—

but because of what I've remembered:

That nothing I hold matters more than who I've become."

And as you cross into the next terrain—from *mastery* to *meaning*—carry this evolved awareness with you like sacred inheritance.

Let your riches be both seen and felt.

Let your wealth be both held and lived.

Let your life—not your ledger—tell the story of your true worth.

The Weight You Cannot Carry

What Patterns in Your Thinking, Your Choices, or Your Past Must Be Released to Rise Further—Into Alignment, Purpose, and Fulfilment?

Before any bird takes flight, it sheds the excess weight.

Before a rocket ascends, it lets go of the spent fuel tanks.

Before a soul evolves, it must confront one painful truth:

You cannot take everything with you.

The higher the calling, the lighter the load.

The Burning Boat

There once was a young seafarer named Veer, known for his unmatched skill at navigating treacherous waters. One day, he heard whispers of a luminous island that only a few had ever reached—a place where time slowed, where clarity reigned, where the soul rested in joy.

Determined, he set sail. But his boat was overloaded—with supplies, memories, trophies of past voyages, and old maps passed down by others who'd never made the journey themselves.

As the waters grew wild and the horizon shimmered with the glow of that fabled island, Veer's ship groaned under the weight. The closer he got to the truth, the more resistance he felt.

Then came a storm—not of wind, but of **inner reckoning**. In its eye, Veer heard a voice, deep and knowing:

"To reach what is real, you must release what is remembered. Not all that brought you this far is meant to take you further."

So, with trembling hands, Veer began tossing things overboard. Old beliefs. Past titles. His fear of disappointing those who taught him well, but wrongly. And then, in a moment of fire and surrender, he burned the very boat that had brought him—swimming the final stretch, naked in spirit.

He arrived not with baggage, but with **becoming**. And the island welcomed him.

The Inner Inventory

We all carry mental cargo—some of it inherited, some self-constructed. But the truth is:

- *Not every belief is a blessing.*
- *Not every success is aligned.*
- *Not every identity is still your truth.*

The rise into alignment and purpose demands sacred subtraction before divine multiplication.

So take stock:

- What assumptions about success were handed to you, not chosen by you?
- What patterns of people-pleasing or overachievement mask an inner void?
- What past wins have become silent prisons you feel obligated to protect?
- What decisions are rooted in fear—of failure, of loss, of being seen?

What must be *blessed and released?*

The Art of Sacred Shedding

Think of a snake shedding its skin—not as a death, but as a rebirth.

Or a tree in autumn—letting go not because it is dying, but because spring is coming.

Even the eagle plucks out its feathers at midlife, retreating into solitude to prepare for flight again.

You too, must become the artist of your own shedding.

Release...

- The need to always be right.
- The loyalty to stories that no longer reflect who you are.
- The idea that growth only comes through struggle.
- The image of perfection that's kept your spirit imprisoned.

A Gentle Reckoning Before the Ascent

Every rise begins with an honest reckoning.

Not a shameful one. Not violent. But tender, sacred, essential.

This is not about rejection—it is about *redefinition*.

It is not about loss—it is about *liberation*.

"Your next elevation is already written in your soul.

But it cannot be read until you unclench your grip on what no longer fits."

You are not who you were. And that is a gift.

Reflection Invitation

As you close this chapter, ask yourself:

- *What inner voices still echo with doubt, and whose are they really?*
- *What identities do I cling to that no longer feel true?*
- *What would my life look like if I stopped performing, and started aligning?*
- *Who could I become if I trusted the future more than I feared the past?*

Because rising is not about climbing higher—

It is about sinking deeper into **who you really are**.

And that next self? That next level of freedom, purpose, and power?

It's waiting.

But only if you let go of the version of you that was never meant to stay.

The Sacred Turning Point

Are You Prepared to Let Ambition Serve Something Greater Than Itself—Your Calling, Your Contribution, and the Legacy Only You Can Leave?

Ambition built the first half of the journey.

But it cannot complete it.

Ambition is the fire that fuels the rise.

But if it burns too long without wisdom, it consumes what it once lit.

And so, after climbing, conquering, acquiring—

you find yourself at a sacred fork in the road.

Not the end.

But a deeper beginning.

The Story of the Unfinished Mountain

There was once a renowned builder named Aarav who spent decades constructing a tower of rare brilliance—each level crafted from skill, sweat, and fierce determination. It pierced the sky, admired by many, envied by most.

But the night before completing the final level, Aarav sat alone under the stars. And for the first time, he didn't feel proud. He felt... hollow.

The tower was high.

But something was missing.

In the silence, his daughter approached with a question not meant to wound, but to awaken:

"Appa(father), this tower is beautiful... but what is it for?"

And suddenly, Aarav saw clearly:

He had built *up*, but not *into*.

He had reached heights, but hadn't yet rooted into purpose.

He had mastered the architecture of success, but not the alchemy of significance.

So the next morning, he began a second creation—not a tower, but a sanctuary.

A space not to impress the world, but to impact it.

Not to be remembered for height, but for *heart*.

From Building to Becoming

This is the invitation now before you—not to abandon ambition, but to **redeem it**.

Let ambition now become a servant, not the master.

Let the energy that once climbed become the river that flows—into people, purpose, and presence.

Because *legacy is not what you leave behind when you die.*

It's what you live into—every single day you love, serve, and align.

The Shift: From Outer Success to Inner Significance

This moment, this *pause*, is not weakness.

It is **reorientation**.

You've tasted mastery.

You've glimpsed wealth.

You've learned the mindsets that shape the powerful.

But now you are being called *home*—to the soul behind the success.

The chapter ahead will ask different questions:

- Not *how much did you gain?*

But *how deeply did you give?*

- Not *how high did you climb?*

But *how fully did you live, love, and liberate others?*

- Not *how rich is your bank?*

But *how wealthy is your soul?*

A Deeper Alignment Is Calling

So ask yourself gently:

- *What if the next season is less about becoming more, and more about becoming true?*
- *What if your greatest impact begins not at the next milestone, but at the next moment of alignment?*
- *What if legacy is not some distant dream, but the echo of how you live today?*

You are standing at the edge of meaning now.

The climb has brought you here.

But only surrender will carry you forward.

Because the next rise will not be defined by numbers, metrics, or applause.

It will be defined by **depth, devotion, and direction of soul.**

The Final Ascent Begins Within

You've built the outer world.

Now step into the sacred work of the **inner world**.

Let the mountain now become a **mirror**.

Let success now meet its purpose.

Let riches now serve their reason.

And as you turn the page into the next book—

know this:

You were not just born to rise.
You were born to rise… into meaning.
Into love.
Into legacy.

This is the sacred journey.

Let us begin.

BRIDGE

From Ambition to Alignment

"You rise highest when your wealth echoes your why and your legacy reflects your light."

— Shree Shambav

Synopsis

You've uncovered the silent forces behind power, understood the true essence of riches, and reshaped your mindset for lasting wealth. But now, a deeper invitation awaits—the shift from external mastery to internal alignment.

This is the threshold where ambition meets purpose, and success demands soul.

It's no longer about what you can earn, but what you are here to embody and leave behind.

The next chapter of your rise is not just about more—it's about meaning.

The Shift from Ambition to Alignment

A soul asks, a legacy listens.

What are you truly seeking—power and riches as ends in themselves, or the freedom, impact, and inner peace they promise?

After walking through the terrain of clarity and mindset, it's time to ask: Is your pursuit aligned with your deepest values, or driven by inherited definitions of success?

There comes a moment in every life—quiet, unannounced—when the outer pursuit slows just long enough for the soul to whisper a question too sacred to ignore:

"What is all this for?"

You've learned how to build power.

You've studied the frameworks of wealth.

You've mastered the mindsets that produce results in the material world.

But now, the terrain shifts.

Power without peace becomes paranoia.

Riches without meaning become a prison.

And success without self becomes suffering in a suit.

We must ask: *Was your climb one of awakening, or one of imitation?*

Are you chasing someone else's dream with your one precious life?

Because at some point, power that is not rooted in love becomes domination.

And wealth that is not rooted in truth becomes a distortion.

You are not here merely to succeed.

You are here to become **whole**.

To let the pursuit itself become sacred.

To let your ambition be guided not by fear or lack, but by alignment.

To turn the fire of ambition into the **light of contribution**.

Are you prepared to let ambition serve something greater than itself—your calling, your contribution, and the legacy only you can leave?

It is not about how high you climb, but how deeply you connect. Are you ready to shift from accumulation to alignment, from achievement to meaning?

This is not a question of achievement.

It's a question of **awakening**.

The game is no longer *how do I win?*

The question now becomes: *What am I here to give? To grow? To heal?*

Can you let go of the scorecard long enough to listen to your soul?

Can you trade the addiction of applause for the serenity of alignment?

This is the sacred threshold.

To rise further, you must first **return inward.**

To align, you must be willing to surrender the noise and listen to the signal.

To create lasting wealth—not just outer—but the kind that *outlives you, enriches others, elevates generations*—you must begin again.

Not as a conqueror, but as a creator.

Not as a seeker of more, but as a steward of meaning.

Where We Go From Here

As **Born to Rise: The Unspoken Principles Behind Power, Riches, and Lasting Wealth** closes, we honour the fire that brought you here:

Your clarity. Your hunger. Your unrelenting pursuit of more.

But now, something greater calls.

Not to abandon success, but to **elevate it.**

Born to Rise: The Sacred Journey from Mastery to Meaning is not a manual.

It is a mirror.

A companion for those ready to evolve from mastery to meaning.

From making a living

*to making a **life**.*

From growth at all costs

*to growth with **grace**.*

From being rich

*to becoming **rich in soul**.*

The climb continues—but inward now.

Welcome to the next ascent.

Welcome to Book Two: *Born to Rise: The Sacred Journey from Mastery to Meaning.*

Life Coach and Philanthropist

Shree Shambav is the visionary founder of the Shree Shambav Ayur Rakshita Foundation (www.shambav-ayurrakshita.org). He founded this institution with a lofty goal: to recognise human identity across gender, ethnicity, and nationality. Through this organisation, he wants to assist all communities in realising their full potential and the intrinsic beauty of life.

Shree Shambav, a Life Coach, is dedicated to supporting people on their journeys of self-discovery and empowerment. He assists people in discovering who they are, determining what inspires and drives them, and overcoming limiting ideas. His approach clarifies what one wants in life, assisting people through goal-setting and a step-by-step process for achieving them. He empowers people to make deliberate and responsible decisions, allowing them to identify their blind spots and evolve as individuals via the use of numerous strategies and tools.

The foundation's bold, uncompromising, and compassionate ventures are always aimed at initiating the "Inner Transformation" process. They focus on spiritual growth, personal growth, and self-healing while emphasising that true progress lies in "Inclusive Growth and Co-existence." This philosophy drives all their initiatives, encouraging a holistic approach to development and well-being.

Under Shree Shambav's leadership, the foundation has launched several impactful movements:

Shree Shambav Green Movement: This mission is to create a healthy, green, and clean earth through responsible water conservation and greening initiatives. The movement strives to make the world a green paradise by encouraging sustainable living and environmental responsibility.

Shree Shambav Vidya Vedhika (Vizhuthugal): This project aims to help students and children by offering training, books, stationery, and uniforms. It aims to provide the next generation with the tools and resources they need to excel both academically and personally.

Shree Shambav and his foundation exemplify the spirit of compassion, transformation, and inclusive growth via their work, which has a profound impact on individuals and communities around the world. His work exemplifies the power of acknowledging and nourishing the human spirit, creating a world in which everyone can reach their full potential and appreciate the beauty of life.

TESTIMONIALS

Journey of Soul - Karma - "We die in our twenties and are buried at eighty." Remember that nothing can stop someone who refuses to be stopped. "Most people do not fail; they simply give up." Shree Shambav deserves full credit. It allowed me to sit and consider what I might miss out on in life. The author has delved into every aspect of our daily lives. How can a seemingly insignificant change in these seemingly insignificant details bring us such joy? The Soul of Journey teaches you the "art of living" as well as the "art of dying."

Twenty + One Series - The rich cultural heritage offered a host in twenty + one short stories with incredible imagination, morals and values prevalent at a given time, influencing how people respond to a crisis or any situation. The author has recreated images with universal values and morals. The plentiful of fascinating from faraway lands would leave the modern play and story writers a cringe. The book supports trust and immeasurable values instilling hope for the new generations.

Death - "Shree Shambav's 'Death - Light of Life and the Shadow of Death' is an extraordinary masterpiece that delves deep into the profound questions surrounding our existence and mortality. The book's opening statement, 'Nothing ever truly dies; it simply ceases to exist in one form before resuming it in another,' sets the stage for a thought-provoking exploration of death's multifaceted nature. Shambav's remarkable ability to navigate the philosophical complexities of death and our universal fear of it is both enlightening and comforting. This book is a testament to the power of understanding and acceptance."

Whispers of Eternity - "Reading 'Whispers of Eternity' by Shree Shambav was a transformative experience that left me captivated from beginning to end. Each section of this exquisite collection delves into the myriad facets of existence, offering poignant reflections on life, death, and everything in between. Shree Shambav's verses are a testament to the beauty of language and the power of expression, inviting readers to embark on a journey of self-discovery and spiritual awakening. Whether celebrating life's simple joys or grappling with the complexities of human emotion, this book is a timeless companion that speaks to the heart and soul of every reader."

Life Changing Journey Series - "Life Changing Journey Series II Inspirational Quotes" is a remarkable collection that illuminates the path to self-discovery and personal growth. With its inspiring quotes and insightful reflections, this book serves as a beacon of light in a world often shrouded in darkness. Each quote offers wisdom, guidance, and encouragement, reminding readers of their inner strength and resilience. A must-read for anyone seeking inspiration and enlightenment.

Learn To Love Yourself – "A Heartfelt Guide to Authentic Self-Love." "Learn to Love Yourself" invites readers on a transformative journey to embrace their true essence in a world often focused on external validation. Through ten insightful chapters, it gently reveals principles of genuine self-love, guiding readers to deepen their connection with themselves. Beyond surface positivity, it encourages the cultivation of resilient self-acceptance, from embracing one's unique qualities to setting empowering boundaries. With inspiring stories and practical wisdom, this book is a trusted companion on the path to inner peace, fulfilment, and joy, helping readers build lives that reflect their authentic selves.

The Power of Letting Go – This book has been a gift to my spiritual journey. Shree Shambav's insights into attachment, personal growth cycles, and forgiveness are enlightening. The concept of seven-year cycles resonated with me, helping me understand the natural phases of life. I feel more empowered to let go of what no longer serves me and step into a life of freedom and fulfilment. A truly beautiful read!

A Journey of Lasting Peace – "A Journey of Lasting Peace" feels like a trusted friend guiding you through the maze of self-discovery. The 18 transformative principles are both practical and deeply resonant, addressing everything from gratitude practices to the art of letting go. Each chapter is infused with warmth and wisdom, making it easy to apply the concepts to my life. I particularly appreciated the emphasis on physical health's connection to mental well-being; it served as a wake-up call for me to prioritise my health. This book is an invaluable resource for anyone serious about personal growth!

Astrology Unveiled Series – "Profound, Logical, and Inspiring". What stands out in Astrology Unveiled is the author's dedication to making Vedic astrology logical and approachable. Each concept flows naturally into the next, backed by examples and exercises. The insights into karma and life cycles add a philosophical depth rarely seen in astrology books. Perfect for anyone seeking spiritual growth alongside astrological knowledge!

The Entitlement Trap - "Thought-Provoking and Challenging" The book challenges readers to confront their own sense of entitlement, and that's not easy—but it's essential. The Entitlement Trap doesn't offer a one-size-fits-all approach. Instead, it's a thoughtful, layered examination of how entitlement can limit our growth. The chapter on "Defining Your Own Hill" was particularly impactful, as it pushed me to reconsider which challenges are truly worth pursuing. A thought-provoking read for those willing to do the inner work to create a life they can be proud of.

Whispers of a Dying Soul – "A Soul-Stirring Reflection on Life's Unspoken Truths" - *Whispers of a Dying Soul: Unspoken Regrets and Unlived Dreams"* is a deeply moving exploration of the unexpressed emotions and unfulfilled aspirations that shape our lives in ways we often don't realise. This book invites readers to confront the powerful, often hidden impact of regret while guiding them through a journey of introspection and healing. Each page opens a space to reflect on the choices that define us—from moments of unspoken love to neglected passions—offering a gentle reminder to live authentically and courageously.

Whispers of the Soul: A Journey Through Haiku - is a mesmerising collection that speaks directly to the heart. Each haiku is a delicate brushstroke capturing life's fleeting beauty and timeless wisdom, inviting readers into moments of deep reflection and peace. This book is a balm for the soul, guiding us to find meaning in stillness and connection in simplicity. The themes of nature, love, and mindfulness echo universal truths, resonating with quiet, powerful grace. It's a book to be savoured slowly, cherished deeply, and returned to often. Truly, a gift for anyone seeking calm and clarity in life's chaos.

Whispers of Silence - Unlocking Inner Power through Stillness by Shree Shambav is a rare gem that beckons readers to pause, reflect, and reconnect with their inner selves. In a world that never stops talking, this book offers a profound exploration of silence—not as a void but as a rich and transformative space.

From the first page, Shree Shambav's writing resonates deeply, blending scientific insights with spiritual wisdom in a way that feels both universal and deeply personal. The author's ability to bridge the tangible and the transcendent makes this book an invaluable guide for anyone navigating the chaos of modern life.

The Power of Words: Transforming Speech, Transforming Lives - "The Power of Words is a profound and enlightening guide that has transformed the way I approach communication. Shree Shambav masterfully uncovers the hidden influence of our words on relationships, self-perception, and overall well-being. This book doesn't just teach you how to speak; it inspires mindful communication that fosters connection and trust. The insights on replacing negative patterns like gossip and judgment with kindness and authenticity are truly life-changing. The practical strategies and engaging narratives make it an invaluable resource for personal and professional growth. A must-read for anyone striving to communicate with intention, clarity, and compassion. Highly recommended!"

The Art of Intentional Living: Minimalism for a Life of Purpose - "The Art of Intentional Living is a refreshing guide to finding clarity in a cluttered world. With practical wisdom and profound insights, it inspires you to simplify, prioritise, and live with purpose. A must-read for anyone seeking balance and fulfilment."

Awakening the Infinite: The Power of Consciousness in Transforming Life - "Awakening the Infinite is a transformative guide that expands the mind and nourishes the soul. With profound insights and practical wisdom, this book beautifully explores the power of consciousness, helping readers connect with their true purpose and inner potential. It is a journey of self-discovery, healing, and spiritual awakening, offering clarity and inspiration at every turn. A must-read for anyone looking to live with greater awareness, meaning, and authenticity."

Beyond the Veil: A Journey Through Life After Death:

"This book touched me in ways few others have—it's not just about death, but about life, meaning, and the vast unknown that connects them. Beyond the Veil offers a graceful blend of science and spirit, inviting us to explore the mystery with awe rather than fear. The stories, insights, and reflections linger in your heart long after the final page. A truly transformative read that brings light on the shadows of mortality. It reminded me that in embracing death, we truly learn how to live."

Bonds Beyond Blood:

"A profoundly moving story that reminds us family is not defined by blood, but by love, sacrifice, and the courage to heal. Every chapter touched my soul with its emotional truth and timeless wisdom. Through joy, grief, and redemption, this book captures the raw beauty of human connection. I saw reflections of my own family in its pages—both the pain and the hope. A powerful, unforgettable read that lingers long after the final word."

A Journey into Spiritual Maturity: 12 Golden Rules for Inner Transformation

"This book is a gentle yet powerful guide that awakened a deeper sense of purpose within me. Each golden rule felt like a mirror reflecting truths I needed to embrace. Shree Shambav's wisdom is timeless, poetic, and profoundly grounding. It's not just a read—it's a journey into the heart of who you truly are. A must-read for anyone seeking lasting peace, clarity, and inner transformation."

The Inner Battlefield: Overcoming the Enemies of the Mind and Soul:

"This book is a powerful revelation—an honest mirror to the battles we fight within. Every chapter is a step closer to clarity, peace, and emotional mastery. Shree Shambav brilliantly transforms ancient wisdom into practical guidance for modern souls. It awakened in me a new strength to face my fears and rise above inner turmoil. A must-read for anyone seeking true inner victory and lasting transformation."

The Seeker's Gold – Unlocking Life's Greatest Treasure

The Seeker's Gold is a soul-stirring masterpiece that goes far beyond the pursuit of wealth—it is a journey into the heart of what truly matters. Each chapter unfolds with poetic wisdom and emotional depth, revealing that life's real treasure is not found in riches but in the transformation of the self. As the protagonist evolves through trials, love, and profound realisations, so does the reader. This book is a mirror for every dreamer, a lantern for every seeker, and a companion for anyone walking the path of purpose. A timeless tale that stays with you long after the final page.

The Power of Manifestation: Unlocking the Path from Thought to Reality

The Power of Manifestation is a profound and enlightening guide that redefines manifestation as a conscious way of living rather than a fleeting trend. With a beautiful blend of ancient wisdom, quantum insights, and spiritual depth, this book gently leads you inward—to the source of true transformation. It empowers you to reprogram limiting beliefs, master your energy, and align with the flow of life, unlocking the creative force within. Each page is a reminder that your dreams are not distant—they are waiting for you to awaken. A must-read for anyone ready to live with intention, clarity, and soulful power.

ACKNOWLEDGEMENTS

To my grandfathers, grandmothers, mothers, fathers, aunts, uncles, neighbours, sisters, brothers, friends, and teachers, they poured in endless moral stories, retellings of Ramayana, Mahabharata, Puranas, Upanishads, and so on.

My teachers, neighbours, and kindred souls. Who provided us with a stage to perform wonderful Puranic stories and were gracious enough to acknowledge our efforts.

The artists and translators of epics have served as a source of inspiration, invigorating our spirits, making these works accessible, and enabling us to grasp the profound depths and deeper dimensions they contain.

I also cherish the stimulating conversations; I had with my wonderful mothers, Punitha Muniswamy and Uma Devi.

Our family's youngest member, Aadhya, who always overwhelmed me with questions, inspired this book.

I would likewise prefer to express gratitude to Mr Sivakumar, Mrs Roopa Sivakumar, Mr Akshaya Rajesh, Ms Akshatha Rajesh, Ms Apeksha Prabhu, Mr Akanksh Prabhu, Mr Nikash Sarasambi, and Mrs Spoorthi Nikash for their valuable inputs.

I must thank Mr Rajesh, Mr Savan Prabhu, Mrs Revathi Rajesh, Mrs Rajani Sarasambi, and Mrs Manju Reshma, who encouraged me and often suggested writing a book. Their unwavering belief that I had something valuable to offer kept me going during my writing sessions.

Love you all,

Shree Shambav

www.shambav.org

shreeshambav@gmail.com

www.ingramcontent.com/pod-product-compliance
Lightning Source LLC
LaVergne TN
LVHW091539070526
838199LV00002B/135